DECORATIVE PAINTING

PAINTING
Flowers
in
Watercolor
with Louise Jackson

NORTH LIGHT BOOKS
CINCINNATI, OHIO

About the Author...

Louise Jackson has painted in a variety of mediums since 1966. Her work today is in watercolor or alkyds. She travels throughout the U.S., Canada and Japan teaching at workshops as well as holding week-long seminars in a studio in Dayton, Ohio. Louise hosted a television series *Painting with Louise,* and has made several videos. She has authored nine other painting instruction books.

In 1991 Louise received her Master Decorative Artist degree from the Society of Decorative Painters. She belongs to several chapters and the Ohio Watercolor Society and the American Society of Portrait Artists.

Her work is in many corporate collections including those of major art supply manufacturers. The Society of Decorative Painters permanent museum collection includes two of Louise's paintings. She also has eight ornaments in the Smithsonian Museum's Christmas collection.

Louise and her husband Ken reside in Centerville, Ohio. They are parents of four and grandparents of three girls.

Painting Flowers in Watercolor With Louise Jackson.
Copyright © 1997 by Louise Jackson. Manufactured in China. All rights reserved. No part of this book may be reproduced in any form or by any electronic or mechanical means including information storage and retrieval systems without permission in writing from the publisher, except by a reviewer, who may quote brief passages in a review. Published by North Light Books, an imprint of F&W Publications, Inc., 1507 Dana Avenue, Cincinnati, Ohio 45207.

Other fine North Light Books are available from your local bookstore or direct from the publisher.

01 00 99 98 97   5 4 3 2 1

Library of Congress Cataloging-in-Publication Data

Jackson, Louise, M.D.A.
    Painting flowers with Louise Jackson / by Louise Jackson.
        p.   cm.
    Includes index.
    ISBN 0-89134-764-X (alk. paper)
    1. Flowers in art. 2. Painting—Technique. I. Title.
ND1400.J3 1997
751.45′ 434—dc20   96-46678
                                                CIP

Edited by Julie Whaley and Kathy Kipp
Designed by Clare Finney

METRIC CONVERSION CHART		
TO CONVERT	**TO**	**MULTIPLY BY**
Inches	Centimeters	2.54
Centimeters	Inches	0.4
Feet	Centimeters	30.5
Centimeters	Feet	0.03
Yards	Meters	0.9
Meters	Yards	1.1
Sq. Inches	Sq. Centimeters	6.45
Sq. Centimeters	Sq. Inches	0.16
Sq. Feet	Sq. Meters	0.09
Sq. Meters	Sq. Feet	10.8
Sq. Yards	Sq. Meters	0.8
Sq. Meters	Sq. Yards	1.2
Pounds	Kilograms	0.45
Kilograms	Pounds	2.2
Ounces	Grams	28.4
Grams	Ounces	0.04

DEDICATION

*I would like to dedicate this book to all of the artists
who have shared their knowledge with me.
Each time I studied with one of them, I came away
with something that became a part of how I paint.*

ACKNOWLEDGMENTS

Thanks to the many sharing teachers in the watercolor
field as well as the decorative painting world. As a
perennial student, I have had many teachers, and because
I love the learning process there will be many
more. Many thanks to Greg Albert for encouraging me
to attempt this book. Thanks also to Julie Whaley for the
many hours spent piecing my notes together into some
semblance of order. As always I thank my husband, Ken,
for his constant support and I thank God who is my source.

Table of Contents

Introduction

Watercolor is a wonderful medium that *can* be controlled. It is no more difficult to learn than oils or acrylics. It is exciting and beautiful as well as challenging and marketable. The best news is, it can be taught in a step-by-step manner.

If you are a moderately experienced painter in another medium, you must temporarily become a beginner again. I say this is only temporary because as soon as you master some of the basic skills, you will find the skills and knowledge that you have acquired with your other mediums will come into play, and you will be using them quickly. You will get better fast.

Remember when you took your first art class and went home with the feeling that "I could improve if I practice." That's how I want you to think as you work through the projects in the book. Don't be afraid to do a project a second or third time. One of my very early pieces was done five times, and I still had to use white to correct something but it got better every time. I love it and it still hangs in my house.

Whether your desire is to paint for pleasure and relaxation, to improve your skills or to decorate your walls, you may enjoy learning my techniques. Perhaps you will incorporate some of these methods with your own for your original paintings.

Know that most watercolorists paint almost every day. The wonderful aspect of it is that it is easy to set it up in a small area and leave it. If you don't have a studio or art room, set it up in your dining room or a corner in a bedroom. Leave your supplies set up in a spot that you can get to when you have an hour to paint. A little painting every day can be very helpful and gives you the needed practice. As long as you cover your paint and empty the water, your materials will be safe even if your cat walks over them.

My recommendation to all students of art is to join your local painting group. Many towns have a watercolor society. Another organization that I highly recommend is the Society of Decorative Painters. This is a group of painters (as students) and artists who teach their original works in all mediums at all levels of instruction. For more information write to:

Society of Decorative Painters
393 N. McLean Blvd.
Wichita, KS 67203

HOW TO USE THIS BOOK

The paintings in this book were created with the idea that you may copy them to learn from them. I want to clarify what you may do with them: First, the drawings are much smaller than the paintings. You may, of course, enlarge them by hand. However, you *do* have permission to take them to a copy center and have them enlarged. You will need to show this passage as it is against copyright law to do this without written permission. Consider this as such.

You also may enter your painting in a show that does not require the work to be original. Always read the requirements carefully to check this.

You may also sell your work with your name on it if you duplicate one of the paintings. However, it would be most appropriate to write under your signature "Original Artist Louise Jackson." It would be unfair to your client to lead them to believe that they purchased a piece of original art.

My wish is that you learn what you need from these techniques. Combine them with yours and develop some wonderful new originals that you won't need to place my name on.

Chapter One: Supplies

Here is an overview of the supplies you will need to complete the paintings in this book.

BRUSHES

You should use what works best for you. If you are an experienced watercolorist, continue to use brushes you are comfortable with. If you are new to the medium, I will describe what I use and why. This may help you obtain the brushes that work best for the techniques in this book.

I use a no. 8 or no. 10 round to apply color to most flowers, and I often use this brush with most of the water removed to blend the edges of color on a wet surface. You'll need a round that maintains its shape and returns to a good point. You may want to purchase a sable brush and, if so, I recommend a Winsor & Newton 720 or 820. It is a reasonably priced sable.

If you prefer a less expensive brush, you may want to try a Midnight Dove no. 10 round. It is made of a new synthetic filament that responds as closely to sable as any I have found. It also has an excellent point and wears better than a sable.

I use a synthetic, short flat (referred to as a chisel blender) for most of my blending. There are only three companies I am aware of that produce a size 20. To

Here are the brushes I use most. Across the top is a double-ended brush (no. 20 flat at left and no. 10 round at right). Then brushes from left to right are: (1) a small scrubby brush; (2) a no. 8 round; (3) a rake brush; (4) a no. 10 flat; (5) a no. 20 flat; (6) a 1-inch; and (7) a 2-inch wash brush.

save you time on your brush-hunting excursion I will list them: Winsor & Newton series 510, Midnight Dove series 104 and Bette Byrd series 300.

Just for convenience, one manufacturer has designed a single brush with a round on one end and a flat on the other. It is easy to apply color with one end and flip it over to blend with the other without having to use both brushes at the same time. For information write to Dove Products Inc., 380 Terrace Rd., Tarpon Springs, FL 34689.

I use a 1-inch flat natural hairbrush for applying background color and softening the colors in large areas. I prefer a Winsor & Newton 295. The plastic handle on this brush is a plus. Do not purchase a brush that has very soft, absorbent hair that soaks up water like cotton. It takes too long to remove the water for blending. Find one that is more like your own hair. Others that work well for my techniques are Winsor & Newton 1-inch Sceptre or Loew Cornell Mixtique.

A good synthetic no. 6 or no. 8 filbert brush is something I use on occasion. I use a Winsor & Newton Regency Gold series 550. Most brush companies have a synthetic filbert in their line and they are easy to find.

You'll need a scrubby brush. I use a no. 4 or no. 6 and a no. 10. The very best are synthetics that are worn to about half their original length. They are used to soften the hard edge of color after masking fluid has been removed and to soften the edges of overlapped color. If you don't have old, worn brushes, you may try a brush with bristles similar to mongoose hair. If it is new, it needs to be slightly stiffer than a synthetic but not as stiff as a bristle brush, as they tend to tear up the paper.

You'll need a script liner or fine rigger brush for fine lines.

Optional Brushes

You will need a tool for wetting large areas. Some artists use a sponge for this. I use a large brush because sometimes I use the same large brush for painting. If you are not going to paint with the brush, the sponge works fine and is certainly less expensive. I use a Winsor & Newton 2-inch flat, series 965. This is a brush that you may want to splurge on as your budget allows.

You may want a no. 10 flat synthetic chisel blender

for small areas. A no. 12 round covers a large background quicker than the smaller round.

Another optional brush is a *rake* brush. As its name implies, it does what a garden rake does. Before these brushes were on the market, I made my own by cutting an old fan brush so it looked like a rake. They are in the synthetic line so they are not too expensive. I use them to paint in streaks or growth lines in flowers.

BRUSH CARE

You may have some brushes that you have used with another medium that will work for watercolor. A good cleaning with soap and water usually will allow you to interchange them if they have been well cared for.

Treat your watercolor brushes, especially sables, as you would your hair. Give them a gentle washing with a liquid soap or shampoo. You may even use a cream rinse on occasion. Rinse well and lay them to dry over your water tub so they are not laying in water (which ruins the handles). You may also hang them to dry so the water drains toward the bristles. When they are completely dry, you may stand them in a container, but if you do this before they have completely dried, the water will run into the handle and ruin it.

When your brush is rewet, it should return to the original shape. I prefer not to leave soap on the brushes because it dries out natural hair bristles.

BRUSH STORAGE

There are many storage containers on the market, or you could simply use a jar, which works fine in the studio. However, if you are painting on location or taking a workshop, a jar may not be the best means for transporting your brushes. You need to have something else for these occasions.

The brushes may have to be put away wet for the trip home so you want to have air circulation. Do not allow the water to drain down into the ferrule or handle. A plastic liner would hold in moisture, so avoid that.

There is one container on the market manufactured by the Dove Brush Company that solves most of these problems. It is shaped like a loose-leaf notebook. The brushes hang down and the air circulates at the wide end of the holder. However, if you have to get on a plane after teaching or taking a workshop, it is best to place a paper towel under the bristles to pull the water away from the handle until you arrive home.

PAPER

My choice is a heavy paper which comes in large sheets—22″ × 30″ (56cm × 76cm). I use many brands and as you go through your watercolor experience, you may want to try as many as possible to find your favorites. I prefer Winsor & Newton Rough (which has a little texture) or their cold-press 260 lb. It is a soft but durable paper with a beautiful white appearance. It is easy to remove colors back to the white paper even when it is dry, unless you are using staining pigments. This is the paper I recommend to beginners because it is so forgiving. It holds the water longer because it is sized both internally and externally, which gives you more blending time.

Lanaquarelle paper has a similar color with one very smooth side and the other a slight texture.

Another paper I use—and one of the easiest to find—is Arches 300-lb. cold-press paper. Or, if you want a smoother surface, try Arches 300-lb. hot-press paper. The Arches dries faster, so you have to work faster to blend. It is also a little more yellow than Winsor & Newton or Lanaquarelle. On occasion the sizing is unevenly distributed. If you get a piece where the paint grabs more in one spot because of uneven sizing, simply paint it into a background. It will show up with the first application of color so, if you are aware of it, you can deal with it. This paper is not as soft as the other two and it withstands more scrubbing. It also takes the color better and may require fewer layers.

There are advantages to each of these papers. You can work with the paper that is easy for you to obtain in your area.

Taping Paper to a Board

You may choose to secure your paper to a thin board with masking tape. If so, you may use a piece of Luan

Tape your paper to a support surface.

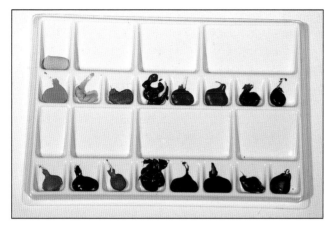

Place the paints on your palette. It is easier to place the colors in the same wells each time you fill the palette. As you become more familiar with them, you will automatically know just where they are.

or door paneling. (Masonite is heavier but it works as well.) Have your lumberyard cut some pieces about 2″ larger than the size paper you will paint on. Sand rough edges and tape them. Tape around all edges of the paper. When removing the tape, do it slowly so the paper doesn't tear.

The board acts as a support, and when the painting is finished, you have a nice white edge around the paper. This shows how it will look with a white mat and the clean edge pleases me. Is this step necessary? No, it is an option.

Until you get a board, you may place a few squares of paper towels under your paper. The first stage in many paintings is wet. The towels will be a reminder to wipe the water off your table as soon as your wet stage is finished. If you allow the paper to dry on a wet table, the water will creep into the edges and create blooms.

Cut your good paper in fourths to practice on. You may use a craft knife or scissors. If you need to cut a lot of pieces, use a mat cutter or take them to your local framer and have them cut for you.

Less Expensive Paper

If your budget is limited you may choose to use a 140-lb. paper. If you prefer this, I would recommend stretching the paper for most of my techniques to reduce the amount of buckling.

Start at the lumberyard and have them cut boards out of luan or door paneling. Get the thinnest they have. Have boards cut for a quarter sheet of paper (11″×15″ or 27.9cm×38.1cm) a half sheet (15″×22″ or 38.1cm×55.9cm) and a full sheet (22″×30″ or 55.9cm×76.2cm). Have the boards cut at least 1″ or 2″ larger than the paper. Sand the edges and tape them

with plastic tape or duct tape.

Cut some of the paper into quarter and half sheets. To stretch the paper, soak it in water for about five minutes. Set it on the board and gently pat it down with clean hands.

At this point, you should be able to use a regular desk stapler to attach the paper to the board while it is still wet. Staple about every two inches. You may work on this immediately or prepare several ahead, allow them to dry and have them ready for the next painting session. This stretching will eliminate about half the amount of buckling normal with a 140-lb. paper.

Using 140-lb. paper costs about half as much as heavy paper, and it will dry faster. But, there are many factors to consider when selecting your papers. These are merely alternatives; you must make the final decision. How will you know what works best for you? There are many fine papers to choose from. Try different kinds. If you use a paper with 100 percent rag content, you won't go wrong.

OTHER SUPPLIES

Water Containers

You will need two water containers (mayonnaise jars work well because they are large and clear). One is for rinsing; the other holds your clean water.

Water Removal Tool

This is what you will use to pull just the right amount of water out of your brush. Some artists use sponges, towels or T-shirts. I use a roll of absorbent bath tissue with four absorbent paper towels wrapped around the roll. I use one per painting.

Watercolor Palette

My choice is a Zoltan Szabo covered palette with slanted wells. You may want to line up the colors on your palette with warms on one side and cools on the other. When you run out of space, you can use the small mixing wells.

Graphite

This is used to transfer the drawing onto the watercolor paper. You need to use a wax-free graphite. There are several brands that are wax free: Sally's, Saral, and Sue Scheewe graphite. Tape the drawing to your watercolor paper in two places to prevent movement. Slip the graphite under the drawing and trace over the lines you feel you need. Many artists prefer very few lines while some artists are more comfortable with everything drawn on. Whatever you choose, if the lines appear dark, you may lighten them with a kneaded

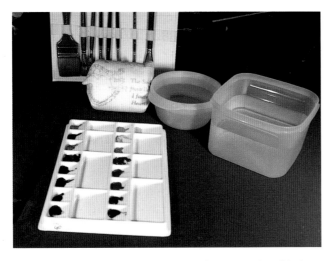

Set up your materials according to what is comfortable for you. When you decide what you prefer, keep it that way each time you paint. You will spend less time locating things.

eraser. If you are going to paint on a wet stage layer, have the lines dark enough so they will show through one light layer of color. Take a piece of your eraser and rub very hard to remove all of the excess graphite.

There are other ways, but I find this the easiest. You may also hold the paper up to a window or use a light-box to trace your drawing.

SETTING UP THE WORK AREA

Set up your work area in this order: Place your two water containers and paper towels near the hand you paint with (either cut a roll in half with a large knife or take about six paper towels and wrap around a roll of bath tissue). It is extremely important to have absorbent towels to pull the water out of your brush quickly.

Set the paper in front of you and your watercolor palette next to it. You need to set things up so you can move comfortably, avoid dripping water on the painting, and begin to get a rhythm with your actions. Your work area should be set up the same each time you paint.

THE HUES OF WATERCOLOR

Color is a wonderful subject. Since this is a "how to" book, I will cover only the colors that are used in it. There are many wonderful North Light books written on the technical and theoretical aspects of color.

Because of their clarity, transparency and color selection, I use mostly Winsor & Newton watercolors. If you prefer another brand, simply identify the colors that are in the paintings. If the names are different, identify them visually.

In watercolor, the transparent colors offer you the opportunity to use layer on top of layer without losing the light-refracting qualities of the paper. Many of the pigments I use are transparent. The three that I use most often are New Gamboge, Permanent Rose and Antwerp Blue. For the first year or so, these were the *only* colors I used. I like to refer to these as the "main three." You can mix any hue with these, even black. I only added more colors because it required less mixing, and it was easier to teach with more colors. If you can only afford three, choose these and mix to what you see. Each mix will contain all three colors.

Mixing Colors

Here is how to use them. Let's say you want orange. Mix the yellow and red. Then, if you want to tone it down, add a touch of Antwerp Blue. What if you want brown? Simply add more blue. How about black? There is a trick to this. Use a palette knife and start with Antwerp Blue because that is the darkest value closest to black. Add a smaller amount of Permanent Rose, a mid value. Then add an even smaller amount of New Gamboge, the lightest value. You can arrive at a beautiful, vibrant black.

If you mix a small amount and prefer to use a brush, use very little water or you will get gray. If you are a beginner and prefer to try watercolors without investing in many colors, you may wish to try this for a while. It will really put you in control of your colors. You will never have to ask someone how to mix a color again.

All the colors I use will lift off most papers. Will they lift back to white? Not all of them, but they will lighten more on these papers than they will on the papers with less sizing. To test the transparency of a new color, simply draw a black line with a permanent marker on your paper. Apply the color over it. If you see the line clearly, that means the color is very transparent. If it covers or appears milky, that means it is more opaque.

With the exception of Yellow Ochre and Naples Yellow these colors are all considered transparent. That means they do not contain white.

The Yellows

New Gamboge is the one that I most often use. It is clear and transparent. It also lifts off the soft papers somewhat. It will not lift off to white paper without scrubbing. New Gamboge is my warm yellow. Most often it is used as a very light wash.

Naples Yellow is milky and only used occasionally.

Winsor Yellow is a cool yellow. It is transparent.

Yellow Ochre is one that is only used on occasion. It is less transparent than most of the other colors.

Reds

Permanent Rose is a most versatile color. It is transparent. Winsor & Newton lists this as a "hard-to-lift" color. I find it lifts easily on their papers.

Winsor Red is referred to as a transparent although when it is applied heavily, it appears opaque. It is a bright red and not easy to lift.

Alizarin Crimson is a red-violet hue. It is a little strong when used straight. When mixed with Winsor Red it produces a cherry red. It is transparent and not quite as clear as Permanent Rose.

Purple Madder Alizarin is a dull, toned-down red-violet. Watered down, it produces soft pinks and added to Alizarin Crimson it tones down the Alizarin Crimson. Mixed with a blue it creates a dark, dull blue. It can be lightened, but is not easy to totally remove.

Permanent Magenta is a fun color that I only use on occasion because the hue is one that is usable straight out of the tube.

Other Colors

Winsor Violet is a color that I use most often to mix with Winsor Green for a dark background when I want it to go from violet to blue to green. When mixed with Winsor Green it produces a blue.

Burnt Sienna is a favorite of mine because when mixed with Antwerp Blue it produces a nice range of dull greens. It will mix everything from an olive to a dull blue-green.

Winsor Emerald is another fun color. It is not transparent, but opaque. I use it only for the wet stage in my florals because when it is used thinly it produces a bright fresh green. It can appear heavy and opaque if used straight.

Winsor Green used very thin can be used in place of Winsor Emerald. It is an extremely strong color to manage but if you can control it you may use it in place of Winsor Emerald. It also makes a wonderful black when mixed with Alizarin Crimson and a full range of greens when mixed with yellows and reds. It is basically Phthalo green in other brands.

If you use white, use white gouache or a new Winsor & Newton color Titanium White (Opaque White).

Blues

Cobalt Blue is a middle value I use for first-stage backgrounds, tints and cools on flowers. When mixed with Permanent Rose it makes a great periwinkle. Mixed with Winsor Emerald it creates a soft grayed green.

Antwerp Blue is basically a blue-green. You will find that it is most often used in this book in a mix with red. The red is the complement of green and neutralizes it. Why not just use French Ultramarine Blue? It is not quite as clean and transparent as Antwerp Blue which also mixes with the Burnt Sienna for my greens.

French Ultramarine Blue has a little sediment, but when you need a strong accent it's great. It also mixes with Burnt Sienna to produce a nice range of browns and grays. One of the reasons I don't have Burnt Umber on my palette is because I prefer to mix my browns with French Ultramarine Blue or the main three (Antwerp Blue, Permanent Rose and New Gamboge).

Winsor Blue is an optional color. It is a darker, more staining version of Antwerp Blue.

Indigo is used only sparingly. It is a dark, toned-down, dull blue.

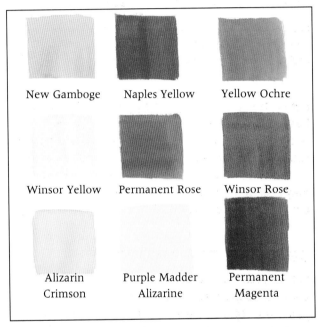

New Gamboge · Naples Yellow · Yellow Ochre

Winsor Yellow · Permanent Rose · Winsor Rose

Alizarin Crimson · Purple Madder Alizarine · Permanent Magenta

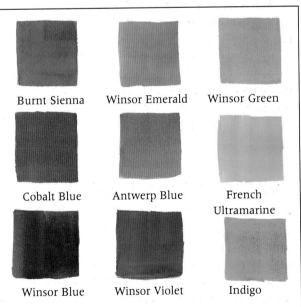

Burnt Sienna · Winsor Emerald · Winsor Green

Cobalt Blue · Antwerp Blue · French Ultramarine

Winsor Blue · Winsor Violet · Indigo

These are the colors on my palette. Check the list of colors used in each painting. None of the paintings use all of these.

Chapter Two: Terms and Techniques

Here are the definitions of the terms and techniques used in the instructions for the paintings.

• **Lift color out**: Use a damp brush. Apply the brush to an area. Allow the water to loosen the pigment and lift the pigment with a thirsty brush.

• **Scrub the edges to soften**: Use a worn-down soft synthetic brush or a scrubber called a Fritch scrubber. Using a damp brush, straddle the hard line that you are trying to soften. Gently scrub up and down along the line. It will move a little pigment into the white area and create another value change.

• **Juicy paint**: This is the color of the full-strength pigment. Use only enough water to make a thick and juicy paint.

• **Wash**: A thin layer of paint applied as evenly as possible. Always work into the wet edge of the paint.

• **Controlling crisp edges**: Aim your round brush to the outside line, and use the point of the brush to achieve a clean edge.

• **Salt technique**: Use only if the instructions mention salt. This may be used in some paintings but not in all. When the paper has lost its shine, that is the time to drop the salt in. Use regular table salt. Let it dry until it is finished working. Use a dryer on it after about ten minutes and then brush off the salt.

• **Using masking fluid**: Coat a wet brush with soap to protect it. Dip brush in masking fluid and paint it on the areas that are to stay white. Work for about five minutes, rinse out your brush and recoat it with soap if you need to mask more. Do not allow the fluid to begin to dry in your brush—it could ruin it. Do not force the fluid dry; allow it to dry naturally. This will only take about fifteen minutes.

• **Remove an error**: Wet the area and allow the water to penetrate the paper. As it does, the pigment begins to float around on the paper. Gently loosen it with a soft brush and blot with a tissue. You may repeat this as many times as needed to get back to white.

• **Mixes**: When there is a + sign between the colors in your instructions that means you should mix the colors together to arrive at the color that you are striving for. You need to determine the color by referring to the painting or photo of the step you are on. When there is a comma or hyphen between colors that means you need to apply each color straight.

• **Dry**: Dry the paper until it is bone dry. You will not feel any dampness to it at all. This means it is dry inside as well as on the surface.

• **Painting negative space**: Think of this as background. After you have painted the wet stage (your lightest values) you may turn some of these colors into leaves. If you paint the background around a leaf shape, then the leaf shape becomes a positive object or shape. The background that you painted color into becomes the negative space.

• **Layering**: To work with a layering method, the most important thing is to dry the paper thoroughly before the next layer. If the paper is not completely dry, the water inside may mix with the new water and create blooms or lines that you hadn't planned on.

• **Blending**: More terms often used refer to blending. Blending the transition line means to remove the color line where you want the values to change gradually.

• **Side loading**: This creates a stroke of color that is blended on the brush. When applied to paper, one transition line is floating into water. Refer to the blending exercise on pages 23-24 for a detailed explanation.

WAYS TO CORRECT A PASSAGE IN YOUR PAINTING

Someone started a rumor years ago that watercolor is the most difficult medium. Each medium demands skills that may take practice to learn. Imagine that you were asked to execute a realistic still life or a realistic portrait in watercolors, acrylics, oils, airbrush or pastels. Do you suppose it would be more difficult for a watercolor artist to do this than an oil painter or an acrylic painter? It is not. It takes *different* skills, not more or fewer.

If you are proficient in another medium and just approaching this one, allow yourself to be a beginner again. All that you know from your other medium will come into play as soon as you master some control of the water. If you are just beginning to paint, don't be bogged down by that rumor. There is no truth to it. Open up and enjoy the process of learning. There may be artists out there who are naturals, but I believe if a person has desire and patience they can learn to paint.

Lifting color.

Scrub edges to soften.

Juicy paint.

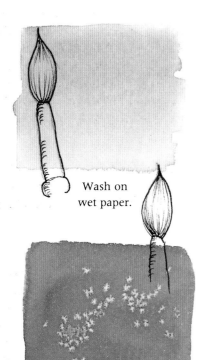

Wash on
wet paper.

Wash on dry paper.

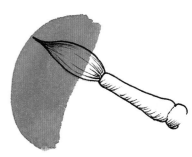

Control crisp edges by
aiming brush to edge.

Drop salt when paper
loses its shine.

Use masking fluid to save small white areas.

Remove an error by
loosening pigment.

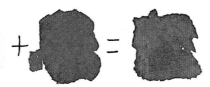

Your notes will have a " + " between colors that
are to be mixed together to produce a new color.

Negative space is the space *around* an object.

Creativity can be developed.

There are more ways to correct or improve a watercolor than you can imagine. I will share those that I know and have used, and together we can search for more.

Although most of these watercolors are transparent, I believe the artist should use whatever works to make a successful painting. If you have a problem that you can't solve in a transparent manner, then use another medium. Eventually you will perfect your skills enough to do a good transparent painting. In the meantime, why live with something that doesn't please you? If you need to use white gouache or white acrylic to restore a passage, please feel free to do so. Today's watercolorists use everything. The purists remain and, while that may be your ultimate goal, do not be restricted by it. If you can't lift or remove it, simply cover it.

Using White Gouache or Opaque White

When you cannot remove any more color and feel the need to lighten an area, you may want to mix a touch of color into white so it doesn't look too chalky. You will find that this blends differently. Even after it dries you may blend a transition line by using a damp brush to loosen the pigment. If you use this in several areas, it is a good idea to mix white with a little background color and paint some in the background. It will look like you intended to use it from the beginning instead of for corrections.

If you are an acrylic painter, you will know how to apply acrylic in several thin layers for corrections. If you are not familiar with acrylics, then use the white gouache or opaque white watercolor. Chinese White is thinner than gouache and takes more layers to cover.

Simply do what it takes to make the painting work. Each time you repeat a painting, your skills will improve. Watercolor is the only medium in which I never minded repeating a painting. Each time I could focus on the technique and see the improvement.

Lifting a Color

If you get a bloom or crawlback or transition line in a spot that you want to remove, dry the paper. Then apply water to the area, and allow it to penetrate the paper for a minute. Take a soft synthetic flat brush and loosen the pigment. Sometimes you want to remove the pigment completely, so blot it with a tissue. Other times you may want to redistribute the pigment by brushing it around and allowing it to dry.

You may repeat this many times, and each time the area will get lighter because you will lift another layer of pigment.

Removing Color With a Stencil

An example of when I might do this is in an area which should remain white. Because scrubbing tends to rough up the paper, I rarely try to put paint over this.

Let's say you are painting a multi-petaled flower and realize that the lightest petals are too dark. Lay a piece of acetate over the flower. Use a permanent marker pen to trace the petal to be restored. Lay the acetate on a surface that you won't damage and use a craft knife or electric stencil cutter to cut out the petal shape. Cut out the ink lines as you cut the shape.

Lay the stencil over the petal to be removed. Take an old soft toothbrush with water on it, and scrub the color off the petal shape. Blot the water on top of the stencil, and quickly lift the stencil and blot the water on the paper or it will run under the stencil. If you absolutely must paint this again, know that the texture of the paper has changed and the paint will absorb differently. Try it and see what happens.

Colored Pencils

Colored pencils seem to work nicely with watercolors and paper. Watercolor pencils are applied like regular pencils. Then water is brushed over the lines for different effects.

Poor Man's Rice Paper

This technique works when a painting is so displeasing to you that you want to discard it. Assemble a mix of equal parts Elmer's glue and water, a sponge and a large piece of inexpensive tissue paper—the kind that you might get in a gift box. Fill the sponge with the glue mixture and gently dab it on the painting, squeezing out the mix. Do not rub the paper or the colors will bleed. Cover the entire paper.

Take the tissue paper and crumble or twist it, and then place it on the paper. You will not be able to move it once it touches the glue. Pat it down, then apply another coat of glue. Allow this to dry overnight.

In the morning, the painting will appear more unified. It will have a rice paper texture. Probably most of what you didn't like will be diffused. It may make a nice little gift—or you might even like it.

You can always cut out the good areas and create very small paintings. Try a mat around an area that you think might be worth saving and see how it looks. Use them as gifts. Your friends will think they are wonderful.

If all else fails, put the paper in a tub to soak a while. Gently remove the color with a sponge. You will end up with a toned paper. It may be dried and used for practice or for a painting with light areas but no white.

When you come up with a new way to save a painting share it with another artist; let's take the fear out of this medium. It can truly be the most fun.

BLENDING EXERCISE

Practice blending with water only. Get familiar with the water in your brush. Learning to judge the amount you are using is what will put you in control.

Load your brush with water, touch the brush to your roll of towels. Allow the thick towels to pull the water out of your brush. Take about half the water out. This is what we will refer to as a 50 percent loaded brush. Do this with each of your brushes. Get to know what a 50 percent loaded brush is. If you are having too much water flow from your brush while painting, adjust your idea about what is 50 percent. Try 60 percent. When my brush is at a 50 percent load of water the wet shine has disappeared from the brush.

The reason I use some brushes that are sable or a mix of natural hair plus synthetic bristles is because the water comes out faster. Think about towel-drying your hair to damp. Now imagine towel drying your hair if it were plastic. Get the idea? It can be done with synthetic brushes; it just takes longer to remove the water.

Now, from each of your brushes remove about 90 percent of the water. This is referred to as a *damp* brush. It is almost dry. Some people refer to it as a thirsty brush.

Step 1. Dip your brush into your clean water container. (Remember, one container is for rinsing your brushes and one is for clean water. *Always* keep this clean.) Take 50 percent of the water out and then pick up color. Set it down on your palette and mix the water and color. Get any lumps out.

Notice the value of this. If you add more *water* it will get *lighter*. This is one way to change values. If you add more *pigment* with a drier brush it will become *darker*.

Take your flat brushes and paint a flat stroke. Try this with each of your brushes. Notice that the water and pigment work together. Watercolors will dry lighter. Next try this with your round brush. Use the round brush on its side and work away from your starting point. Play with it and see what happens.

Step 2. Use the flat brush and paint an area only 1″ long. Quickly rinse your brush, reload it 50 percent with water, and apply to the edge of the stroke to soften the transition line. Straddle the line—place the brush half on the line and half on the clean paper. This deposits water on the paper for the line to move into and fade. It will not go farther than the water.

I use a short choppy, overlapping stroke rather than trying to do it in one long stroke. *Practice.* Then try the same with a round brush. This is an important skill, so practice it until you have mastered it.

It is important to stress that even a tiny amount of color in your clean container can mark the paper. This is true especially when your final blending is into white paper.

Step 3. Side loading with watercolor is a little different than with other mediums but the goal is the same. You want to load the brush so the stroke has color on one side and fades gradually across leaving no line on the other side. Here's how: Mix a puddle of medium-value paint. Holding the brush in a horizontal position with the bristles in a vertical position rather than flat, touch the brush side into the mix so just about six hairs at the outside edge pick up the color. Touch this flat to your palette edge and it will start the flow across the brush. Now set and pull down on your paper. Try it several times. Reclean and reload each time.

If you had problems, check if you are using a 50 percent loaded brush. If it bled too much, try a little less water. If your brushes are all synthetic, it will take longer to get the water out of the brush.

When you have mastered this skill, try the next. Load your brush the same way. Set it down and make a stroke; then pick up the brush, overlap the last stroke and pull it down again. Repeat and repeat on the same stroke. This deposits a larger area of color and still fades out at the edge. I refer to this as "walking the color over." Practice this with all of your flat brushes, especially the 2-inch. The hard part is over. If you can master these skills, the rest is a piece of cake.

Step 4. Use a no. 10 or no. 12 flat bright and paint some chisel edge lines. Quickly clean and reload this time to a damp brush (which means take about 90 percent of the water out). Now take the damp brush and chisel between the lines on the paper. They should bleed, but not become smooth. This should create the look of several values and create what is called *texture* in watercolor. If it got too dry, try again with a tad more water. Only paint 1″ at a time on anything you want to blend or the paint will dry too fast to blend.

Step 5. Apply paint in the manner shown to an area no larger than shown with a round brush. Get a 50 percent load of clean water on your round and touch it to all the edges, allowing the pigment to bleed into the water. This will create lots of value change. It is a fun way to create texture or a streaked look to flowers. The brush is moved back and forth horizontally.

1. More water = lighter values. More pigment and less water = darker values.

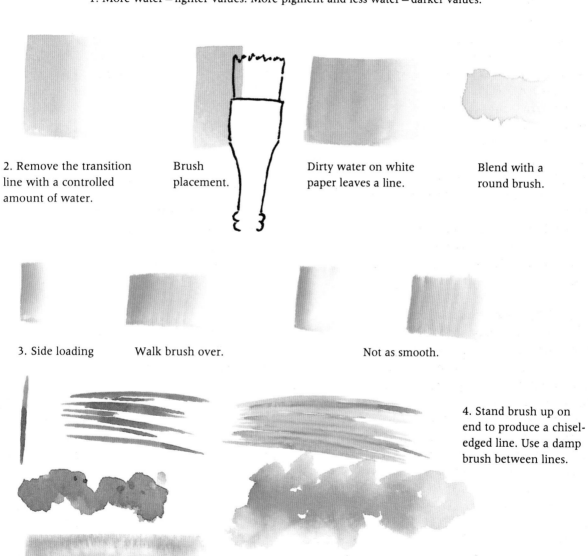

2. Remove the transition line with a controlled amount of water.

Brush placement.

Dirty water on white paper leaves a line.

Blend with a round brush.

3. Side loading

Walk brush over.

Not as smooth.

4. Stand brush up on end to produce a chisel-edged line. Use a damp brush between lines.

6. Wet an area, add color, and watch what occurs. Repeat and use a damp brush to soften some edges.

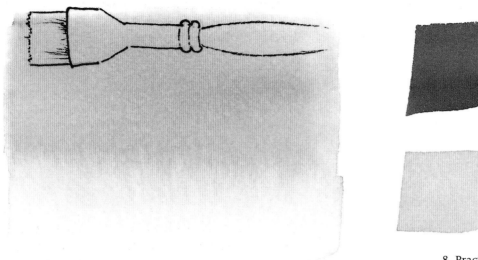

8. Practice controlling the values with water.

7. Try a wash. If you run out of paint, observe that it will get lighter.

9. Use your round brush point to create narrow lines.

10. Paint on a line—use a damp brush to soften the end of it.

11. To paint a solid block, work into the wet edge. Starting in the center and painting out will not produce solid color.

12. Side load until you can do it easily.

13. Try lifting color off damp areas . . . and dry areas to learn what your paper does.

Step 6. Wet a 2" rectangle, and then apply some paint with a flat. Watch what happens to it. Wet another rectangle, apply paint at the bottom with a round and observe. Do this several times. Then take your flat, damp brush and after the pigment has run, soften the edge. Familiarity will cancel out any fear.

Step 7. Try a wash. This is a fairly smooth wash. Wet the paper twice until it is evenly soaked. If it is very wet, you will have a longer working time. If it starts to dry before you are finished, you must stop. If you are painting and your paper begins to lose its shine or its wet look, simply stop. Dry with a hair dryer, rewet and begin again. The paint underneath will not move if it is bone dry. If you work in an area that is starting to dry, you will not be able to get smooth blending.

Wet the paper and load your 2-inch damp brush (90 percent of water removed). Pick up color and apply the paint from the left side to the right. Repeat as you move down the paper.

If you go over an area take a little more water out on your towel. Each time you touch into a wet area, use a drier brush. If you add more water, it will run. After you have done a couple washes, put a few drops of water on them to see what happens. Notice the amount of running depends on the dryness of the area.

Step 8. Practice getting several values by varying the amount of water.

Step 9. Practice using your no. 8 round up on the point to create thin lines.

Step 10. Paint a dark line about 1½" long with a dark value. Touch the bottom edge with a damp brush. This is used to add in dark thin edges where you might desire a strong color.

Step 11. When you want to cover an area solid—for instance, to paint a square—start at one side and work away from the starting point. The wet area is constantly being touched by the new paint and this creates a smoothness. If you outlined a square and worked to the center, by the time you arrived at the center, the first area you had painted would be drying, and you probably would get a bloom where wet and dry met.

Step 12. Practice side loading and walking the brush over again.

Step 13. How to remove an error. Paint an area and, as soon as the shine is gone, take a damp brush and lift out the color. If you want to remove something that has set, first you must dry the paper thoroughly. Wet the area and let it set for a minute. With a wet brush, loosen and lift the pigment. Blot with a tissue. When this is dry, lift another spot and blot.

Get to know your paper and know how far back to white paper you can get if you need to remove something. The Winsor & Newton paper is sized inside as well as outside which means that you can remove non-staining pigments all the way back to white paper. The Lanaquarelle paper is similar. The Arches papers will lighten a lot, but not quite as much, however, it is sturdier.

The trick is this. Place water on the area to be lifted. Allow it to set a minute. The pigments will begin to float around in the water a little. Take a damp, soft brush and loosen the pigments more. Blot with a tissue. You may do this many times over and over. Each time it will lift more color.

If I could show you these techniques in person they would seem easier, but truly if you practice them a few times, you will gain all the control to execute the paintings we will do in the upcoming lessons.

Chapter Three: Worksheets

This chapter includes the basic techniques that were used to execute the paintings in this book. If you spend a little time practicing them, you will gain control of the water. Allowing the water to act spontaneously produces exciting results. However, before you take this direction, learn to control or guide the water and the color for a successful painting.

These exercises are invaluable. In the painting instructions it is assumed that you have practiced these steps, so you may have to refer to them often.

BLENDING WORKSHEET

Blend a Transition Line

When you apply a color on a subject and wish it to gradually fade to no line, you have several choices (see 1, 2 and 3). If you are working on dry paper, you may use a no. 20 flat with about half of the water removed. Position your brush so it is touching the edge of the color. Straddle the line. Set it flat on the paper so it is depositing water along the side of the line. The color will flow until it hits dry paper, then it will stop. This is the reason that you want to use a brush that is at least as wide as a no. 20. I use short, overlapping strokes. They are done as if you are caressing the paper. Allow the water to do the blending.

To remove a line on a wet surface, simply use a much drier brush. (I refer to this as a thirsty or damp brush.) Remove as much water from it as possible. It should feel as you would if you towel dried your hair until it was just damp.

You may choose to blend with a round brush in the same manner.

Creating Streaks

Wet the petal with water (see 4). Apply the color with the round and then clean the brush. Remove the water to a damp stage. Place the brush along the edge of color and pull toward the center then out toward the edge, directing the color. Try and leave the bulk of it where it was first placed. Remember that you are just directing the color. Allow the water to do the work.

Side Loading

Most often this will be done on dry paper. If you choose to do this at the damp stage, simply use less water. Remember that more than half of the brush will carry water.

Mix the color in a thick puddle. Use the largest flat possible. Fill the brush with water. Remove half of the water, and dip the side of the brush into the color. For the color to begin to fade across the brush, you must touch it once to something. It can be the edge of the palette or a damp area on your paper towels.

Set the brush flat on the paper and pull overlapping strokes, again caressing the paper. This blends your color with little effort if you can master it.

Look at illustration 5. The two strokes on the left (top and bottom) were done with the 1-inch brush. Notice how they fade to the right. The two in the center show you some possible problems. The top one shows you what happens when the color travels all the way across the brush. It creates another transition line. The bottom one gives the appearance of a dark line to the left, caused by too much water pushing the pigment to the edge. The two on the right are done correctly with the size no. 20 (they fade to the right).

1

2

3

4

The illustrations on the far right were blended with a round brush.

Covering a Large Area With a Round Brush

This is something you might do on a background. It could be a solid black background or a background with color changes. Decide on a starting and stopping place. Perhaps there is a leaf that touches the edge of the paper or a petal that reaches off. If you are working toward a smooth background this is important. If it is not smooth, then don't concern yourself.

Begin at the edge of the subject (see 6). This is a good way to clean up edges. Use the round brush as if you were mopping a floor. Use the belly of the brush on the paper. As you work away from the subject you are creating wet edges. As much as possible, try and work the next brush load into the wet edge. As you will see, it is best to work in one direction, and it's easier if you have a starting line that you don't have to blend.

Since you can't work to the right *and* left, you may want to blend one side with water. That way it won't form a hard line before you get back to it.

Painting a Dark Background With a 1-Inch Flat

Use thick, juicy paint. Fill the brush and pull a few strokes about an inch long (see 7). Make the strokes on an angle as if you were going to make an *x*.(Don't actually make an *x*—that just gives you the direction.) Each time you fill the brush, change the color. Allow each color to merge. If you want this very dark, it may have to be done twice.

Chisel Blending

Many times I use this when painting something like a long tulip leaf. Apply the color with a flat brush (see 8). Leave lots of white paper. Prepare the flat brush so it carries about 50 percent water. Chisel into the edge of the color, directing it the length of the leaf.

Using a Rake Brush

Fill the brush all the way to the ferrule. If you paint on dry paper it may appear harsh (see 9, left). However if you take this same brush and, while the pigment is still wet, brush over it with a 50 percent loaded brush, it will appear softer (see 9, right).

Lifting Color

To create leaf veins or form a leaf, start with a very dark base on the leaf. Lift the veins using a chisel edge on a dampened flat brush. If you want to actually lift more color out to create form, you may use the same brush. If you have a short, worn-down brush this works even better (see 10).

Most oil painters do what is called a rub-out painting. That is where the colors are placed on, then the values are created by lifting or rubbing off color. This is the same principal. Use water on the brush to loosen the pigment and lift off the color.

WET STAGE WORKSHEET

Many paintings have what is called the wet stage. It is a layer of color used to tone the paper. When these colors dry, they become the lightest colors on the paper. This may end up as soft color in the background. It may provide tints on the flowers and leaves.

Wet the paper until it is evenly soaked. Allow the water to penetrate the inside of the paper. Apply your colors with a large, flat brush. With a damp, thirsty brush, soften the edges where the colors meet. When the paper has lost its shine, dry it with a hair dryer until it is bone dry. Soak up any water that might be on your table or support board so it will not run back as your paper dries.

To do layering, the most important thing is to dry the paper thoroughly before applying the next layer. If the paper is not completely dry, the water inside the paper may mix with the new water you apply and create blooms or lines that you don't want.

Dropping Salt

If the instructions direct you to do this, here is how: When you have blended the colors of the wet stage, watch the paper dry. If you want little stars, drop salt as the paper begins to lose its shine. If you want larger holes, perhaps for foliage, drop the salt when the paper is very wet. Use regular table salt.

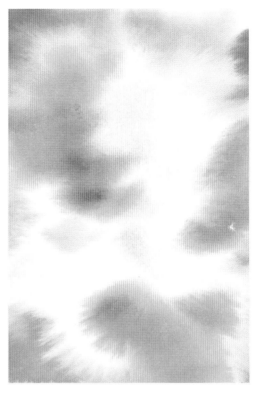

This illustration shows where the color is applied. This is on dry paper simply so you can see it.

This shows the same colors applied to a very wet paper. Soak paper until the water is inside. It will be glistening.

This shows the same application with the edges of the colors softened. To do this, take a clean, damp brush and gently pull at the edges of the colors to soften them together.

The lower right shows a little salt dropped, just as the paper begins to lose its shine.

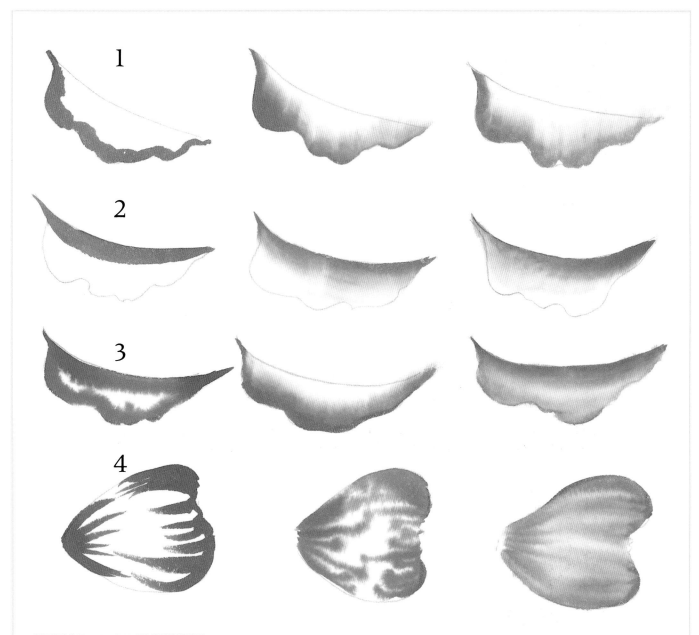

PETAL WORKSHEET

Illustration 1, left, shows the color placement applied to roll a petal down. The center illustrates the look that is achieved when you blend a color with a no. 20 flat with 50 percent of the water removed. The right was done with a side loaded no. 10 flat.

Illustration 2 shows the color placed at the top. This will roll the petal in. The second shows the blending on dry paper. The third shows you the look that you may get using a round brush to blend the transition line.

Illustration 3 shows what the petal looks like when it is wet first, then has the color applied. Some artists are able to blend this easily, keeping the center light. If you have difficulty, simply apply the color to one edge and blend. Dry the petal and then proceed to the other edge. Wetting the paper first makes it easier to blend. However having that layer of water down first will lighten the value. Make your mix darker to compensate.

Illustration 4, left, shows the color placement for streaks. The center shows you what it may look like on a wet surface. The right shows how this simple application can produce growth lines and texture to a petal. After the color is applied to the wet petal, use a damp round brush to direct the streaks.

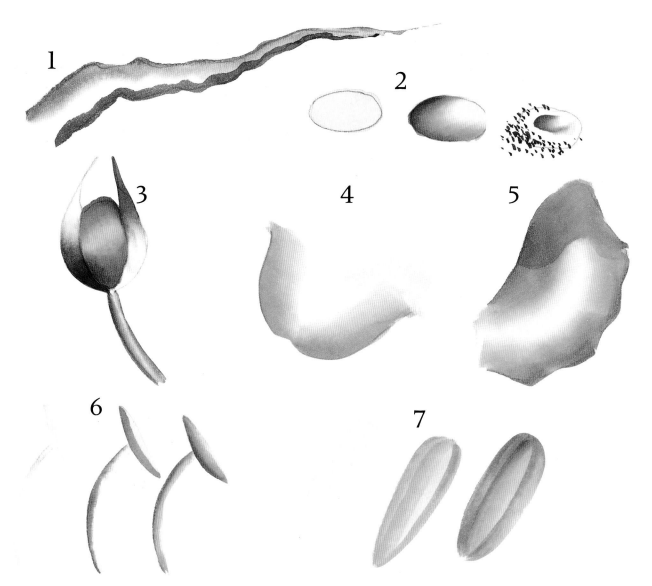

WORKSHEET FOR BRANCHES, STAMENS AND SHADOWS

Illustration 1 is a branch. At the top of the branch you see how it looks when the color is blended. The bottom shows you how much color to apply.

Illustration 2 is a flower center that is often used for daisies and zinnias. Base the center yellow and allow it to dry. Side load Alizarin Crimson around the side. It should look like a *c* (center).

Some flowers have a recessed area which can be indicated with a smaller *c* shape. Pollen on a daisy may fall onto the petals as well as be near the center (right).

Illustration 3 shows how to create a bud shape. Apply dark color at the top and bottom of the bud. The calyx (at left and right) can be darkened at the top and bottom, leaving the center lighter. Stems should be kept light in the center to create a cylinder.

Illustration 4 shows how to create form on a petal with a bowl shape. Simply darken at one or both sides.

Illustration 5 shows how to paint a shadow. Remember that a cast shadow does two things. It reflects the shape of the object that is casting it. It also reflects the form of the object that it falls on. Soften the edge just a little with the tip of a damp round brush. You want it to soften a tad but not move. In reality, the shadow is the color of the object that it falls on, but I often use a shade of another temperature just to create interest, such as the purple shown here.

Some stamens need to have several values to them (see 6). The larger they are, the more values they need.

The elongated buds in illustration 7 are easily done by side loading a no. 20 flat, or painting in the value changes and blending the transition lines. You may need to allow each to dry before applying the next.

LEAF WORKSHEET

Illustration 1 shows a leaf that was based with a thick, juicy mix of Winsor Green and Alizarin Crimson. When it dries, lift out the veins with the chisel edge of a damp, flat brush.

The leaf in illustration 2 was based with the same mix. Use a damp, flat brush to lift out the color. Start at the outside edge of the leaf and work toward the vein area. Lift the color and wipe the excess off of your brush.

Base the leaf in illustration 3 with New Gamboge. With the chisel edge of a no. 20 flat brush, paint in a dark mix of Antwerp Blue and Burnt Sienna. Chisel color to the top and bottom. Quickly rinse the brush and remove most of the water until it is a damp brush. Pull the color or direct it lengthwise on the leaf.

The holly leaf in illustration 4, left, was based dark and the veins lifted out. The one in illustration 4, right, was based the same, and the dark was side loaded in.

Illustration 5 shows a basic leaf shape. The front side (right side) had the color applied to the outside edge and the transition line was blended. I left a light area to create a roundness or roll to the leaf (see above right). The back (left) side had some dark painted in the area above the vein. This was dried.

The vein look on this was created by side loading darker pigment. Start at the outside edge of the leaf and walk the brush over toward the vein. There are three strokes next to the leaf showing paint added to the area above the vein.

Illustration 6 shows the procedure for creating form in the leaf. Base the leaf and dry it. Paint on the colors as you see them placed—one at a time—and blend out the transition line.

This is the form that I most often use. It is very basic. You may choose to use tints and accents as well as stems, tears, flips and veins.

This worksheet has some small leaf shapes in the center to practice as well.

Chapter Four: Simple Projects

This chapter includes several different methods of painting flowers. I hope some of the techniques will help you find new ways to render flower petals and leaves. I suggest that you start with the leaf-negative space exercise. Once you do this you will not have a problem understanding the negative space concept.

The tulip study provides an exercise in creating some basic petal forms and following growth lines.

The rose painting is a very controlled method of painting a complicated subject.

The wild roses provide a study of controlling growth lines, rolled petals, negative shapes, leaves, buds and centers.

1 Trace the leaves on a small— 6½″ × 8″ (17cm × 20cm) piece of paper—Use the same type of paper you will paint on.

Painting Negative Shapes

This is probably the most valuable exercise you can do. Like me, you may resist doing it. However, it really is worth the little time it will take.

I used the following watercolors by Winsor & Newton: Winsor Emerald, Antwerp Blue, Burnt Sienna, Permanent Rose, Purple Madder Alizarin.

This is not a leaf study, but you may turn it into one by painting some of the leaf shapes. Refer to the leaf study worksheet in chapter three.

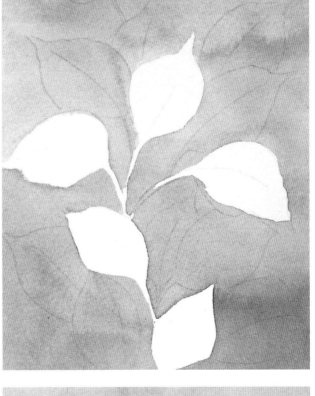

2 Paint a wash of Winsor Emerald over the entire paper. Dry this until it is bone dry.

3 Paint around all of the leaves that have *A*s on them. You may do this with a 1-inch flat or a round brush. Use a green mix made with Antwerp Blue + Burnt Sienna. Dry completely. Notice as you apply each layer that the paint underneath does not move. That is why it is important to dry the paper so thoroughly.

4 Paint around the *B* leaves. Use the same mix. Even though you won't darken the mix, it will become a little darker simply because it is another layer.

5 This time change your mix to a blue made with Antwerp Blue + Permanent Rose. Paint around the *C* leaves. Dry again. Soften the edges of any hard-edged leaves using a small flat, *damp* brush.

6 Now you may get creative and make up your own shapes. You can do it! Paint in a dark mix near the center. Use a dark blue mix made with Antwerp Blue + Purple Madder Alizarin. These will be your darkest shapes. Continue around the design creating more shapes by painting the space around them with the same mix plus a little more water. Go around the entire design twice. I promise you that you will have a very good understanding of painting negative space around positive objects once you have experienced this.

Spike Flower

Supplies

Paper: 11″×15″
(27.9cm×38.1cm) Winsor &
Newton 260-lb. cold-press.

*Winsor & Newton
Watercolors:* New Gamboge,
Purple Madder Alizarin,
Cobalt Blue, Yellow Ochre,
Burnt Sienna, Winsor Green,
Winsor Violet and Antwerp
Blue.

Additional Supplies: Winsor
& Newton Art Masking Fluid
and a Stylus.

1 Wet paper thoroughly. Paint in New Gamboge, Purple Madder Alizarin, Cobalt Blue and Yellow Ochre in background as instructed in Wet Stage Worksheet (see pages 25-26). While the paper is damp, place Purple Madder Alizarin on the blossoms of the flowers and some spikes.

If you are able to continue painting on the drying paper without adding too much water, you may paint the leaves and spikes that are defined on the drawing. If you are a novice at controlling the water, then let the paper dry before beginning the leaves.

Paint a green wash on one leaf at a time. Use a mix of Antwerp Blue + Burnt Sienna to make a green. Take a stylus and indent the veins as if you were writing on paper. The paint will gather in the lines making them appear dark. It is a very easy way to make veins. The leaves need darker values of the same mix. It is best to dry them before painting dark values. Dry the whole paper thoroughly.

2 Apply masking fluid to all the blossoms, leaves, spikes and a few tiny stems. Allow this to dry naturally.

After the masking fluid is dry, rewet the whole paper. Now begin to play. Paint in the leaf shapes. Begin at the outside of the design, because these will bleed and lighten the most. Get darker close to the flower. Remember, to get darker use less water in your mix.

Play with your brushstrokes. Make them into leaf shapes. Try the 1-inch flat, the no. 20 flat and the no. 8 round brush. Use a variety of mixes made from Antwerp Blue + Burnt Sienna as well as Cobalt Blue + Yellow Ochre. Also try a few Cobalt Blue leaves.

As the paper dries, add a darker value using a mix of Winsor Green + Winsor Violet to make a very dark green. Dry the paper and add some smaller dark green leaves throughout. Dry the paper again.

3 Remove the masking fluid.

4 Take a small, worn scrubby brush and dip it in clean water. Remove excess water by touching it to a paper towel. Run the damp brush along all the edges where the masking fluid created a hard-edged look. Soften lines with a gentle scrubbing motion. This does work some of the background color into the flower. Do this step on the long spikes as well. Do not soften the tiny stems. Leave them crisp.

5 Spatter some color. Strengthen darks if needed. Paint more details on leaves. Strengthen pinks on flowers. Here's the completed painting.

Simple Tulips

Backlit Pink Rose

Supplies

Brushes: Winsor & Newton no. 20 Regency Gold 510, no. 8 round sable, 1-inch series 295, no. 8 CJAS Fritch Scrub 77F—special scrub brush or worn down scrubby brush.

Paper: Arches 300-lb. hot-press or stretched, 140-lb. cold-press. Art Masking fluid.

Winsor & Newton Watercolors: Permanent Rose, Alizarin Crimson, Purple Madder Alizarin, Cobalt Blue, Winsor Violet, Winsor Green, Ultramarine Blue.

Mask off all M-areas.

© 1994

This is a map to help you follow the step-by-step directions.

There is some layering on this with some strong application of color. Everything that is painted on is blended or allowed to blend itself. I like to try to allow this to happen. When it doesn't quite blend as I would like, I use a damp brush to direct it.

This is best if you work one petal at a time. Skip around so you give the last one time to dry before wetting the one next to it.

Mask off sections of the drawing marked *M*. Use masking fluid and remember to use lots of soap on your brush before picking up the fluid. Work about five minutes, then clean and reload the brush again. Allow this to dry naturally then do the following:

A. Wet the upper left petal (small one) with thin Permanent Rose to the left and Cobalt Blue + Permanent Rose to the right. Because of the masking that separates these, you may paint the large one below it.

B. Paint Permanent Rose to the right and Cobalt Blue + Permanent Rose to the left.

C. Paint a wash of Permanent Rose on the inner bowl petals and allow to dry.

D. For the petal that is upper far left: Paint on Permanent Rose to outside and a mix of Purple Madder Alizarin + Alizarin Crimson to inner portion.

E. For the large bowl shape: We want to get this dark quickly. Wet the bowl with Alizarin Crimson and as you move to the right pick up Purple Madder Alizarin with the Alizarin Crimson to deepen. Before you begin, observe that the round part of the bowl is lightest. Use a little more water in the Alizarin Crimson here, or lift a little while it's still damp.

F. Repeat this in the partial bowl shape just above

this. Paint Alizarin Crimson + Purple Madder Alizarin to the strip of paper not masked above this.

G. Paint this same mix directly on the petal left of the inner bowl. Allow to dry, then come back and paint the same mix at the bottom of the small inner bowl next to it. Make this a little darker. Blend upward. If petals are not separated in this area, do so now.

H. The last petal near the bowl is next. (We are saving the three largest ones for last.) This petal can be done in two stages if it is easier for you. Paint on a small band of Permanent Rose near the masking. Add Cobalt Blue + Permanent Rose next and a mix of Alizarin Crimson + a tiny bit of Purple Madder Alizarin last. If you can't handle three areas, let the petal dry and add the dark later.

I. For the large petal on right: Wet the petal with a wash of Permanent Rose. Add Purple Madder Alizarin + Alizarin Crimson to recessed areas. Notice where the petal turns down in a strong manner. The dark color was blended but held where it was placed. Keep the brush pretty dry to blend. If you prefer, do the Permanent Rose layer first and let it dry. Then do the darker layer. This turned area will need to be done a second time regardless of how you paint it. Dry completely, then repeat.

The darkest area may need two layers as well. Begin by applying color closest to the darkest area outside the bowl. Hold the edge of color at the bend. Deepen, dry and deepen again. Paint a smaller dark with Purple Madder Alizarin. It is difficult to judge the rose while the masking fluid is on it. Check the values against the photo of the finished piece.

J. For the large lower petal on the left: Wet this petal

Each petal of a rose has its own personality. Each lifts and rolls a little differently. Follow the directions in the text for *A* through *F* for these petals. (The letters coordinate with the drawing.) Observe how you are trying to turn each one.

Here's a close-up of *G, H* and *I*. The large petal to the right is probably the most interesting because it has many shapes within it.

Begin working on the larger petals. To keep the *J* petal light, it is important to wet the petal before applying the pigment. The darkest value of the *K* petal will probably need two layers. Be certain the first one is dry before adding the second.

so it will stay light. Start on the left edge with Permanent Rose, and add the red mix in the dark area. Direct it with the thirsty brush, and paint a small amount of the red mix on the lowest folds. Fill in the small patch to the right of the masking fluid with thin Purple Madder Alizarin. Check the large bowl. If it's not dark enough, paint another dark layer with Purple Madder Alizarin + Alizarin Crimson. Dry.

K. Now to the large cool petal in front. You want to make this look as if it is coming up like a cup (the dark red). It should be lightest facing the sky, and cool because the light is from the back. It also needs to roll down at the edge. Use Alizarin Crimson + Purple

Madder Alizarin to create dark. Blend the edge but hold it there. Use the damp tip of the round brush to touch the color edge. Dry thoroughly. Start at outside bottom edge with the red mix. Paint a Cobalt Blue layer on the cool roll. Dry this, and add another layer of red mix in the dark area.

L. Start on left side of background. Use a juicy mix of Winsor Violet plus Winsor Green. Alternately, pick up more green and do a few strokes, then violet, then a few more green, then Ultramarine Blue. Use a 1-inch flat and very juicy paint. Paint on a few strokes in one direction, always overlapping the wet edges. Work around the entire rose. Use more green as you come

It is important to use a strong dark in the large petal to the right. The dark red at the bottom of the *K* petal helps it to roll downward. The tiny darks added to the small inner bowl petals help to separate them.

This shows the thick, juicy paint you need to use on the background. When it is dry, you may lift out leaf shapes with a damp brush. Keep the leaves simple. With the exception of a few, just create overlapping shapes by painting another layer of the same colors to the negative space between them.

around the lower right side. It still needs some Winsor Violet with it, as it is too intense when used alone. Dry this.

M. Remove art masking fluid with a rubber cement pick-up or eraser, or gently roll it off with clean fingers.

N. Take your clean scrubby brush, dip in clean water, blot and soften all edges of white. Soften the pink sides first, then the dark side touching the background.

O. Use mix of Alizarin Crimson + Purple Madder

Alizarin to separate inner bowl petals. Paint in small, dark triangle shapes and blend out transition line.

P. Make black with Alizarin Crimson + Winsor Green. Begin to create some positive leaves on the background as well as negative space around lower right leaves.

Q. Use a nib or brush with a good chisel edge to lift out veins. Just get a value change without getting it too light.

Wild Roses

1 Follow the instructions in the Wet Stage Worksheet on pages 25-26. Use Winsor Emerald, Cobalt Blue and a mix of Winsor Red + Burnt Sienna. As the shine diminishes, paint Winsor Red on the flower petals leaving some areas white. Use the 1-inch flat brush for this. Paint New Gamboge on the flower centers and on the petal on the right flower that will roll forward.

As the paper dries, the color will bleed less. Using an even drier brush, paint in Burnt Sienna + Antwerp Blue mixed to a green on some of the leaves. Add Winsor Red on a couple leaves for the veins. Use a liner brush for this and very little water.

2 Wet one petal at a time with water. On the left petals, use mostly Winsor Red; on the right petals use Winsor Red + Purple Madder Alizarin mixed as well as Winsor Red straight. Using a large round brush, apply paint to outer edge of petal, pulling a few strokes inward. Direct the color with the rake brush. To soften and the growth lines, fill the rake brush with water. Remove half the water and pull the brush inward.

3 Add tints or washes of New Gamboge to the flowers. Paint the undersides of rolled petals, where you see the back, with a mix of Winsor Red + Purple Madder Alizarin. These are small dark areas on the painting.

4 Develop leaf shapes in the background. Paint around the drawn leaves and create some of your own. (The drawing is only a guide. When you get comfortable enough, make them up as you go.) Use a variety of mid-value mixes. Use Ultramarine Blue + Burnt Sienna mixed cool, then mix it on the warm side. Also use a green mix of Antwerp Blue + Burnt Sienna (the mix I used most). Paint in dark values to some leaves with a thicker mix of Burnt Sienna + Antwerp Blue.

Paint the leaf portion of the bud with this same mix. At the bottom of the bud in the flower portion, paint in a mix of Winsor Red + Purple Madder Alizarin. Blend the transition line with a flat brush with about 50 percent of the water removed.

5 Continue painting the other petals. Locate the petal on the right flower that rolls forward. You should have painted a yellow wash on the bottom underneath portion. Wet this and apply some Winsor Red to the bottom and direct it upward with a clean, damp brush. Allow some of the yellow to show. When this dries, darken the bottom of the part of the petal that rolls forward with Purple Madder Alizarin + Winsor Red.

Iris on Black

Backlighting provides the possibilities of a dramatic effect. I reconstructed a finished painting to provide this lesson. The shapes in the steps may vary slightly—ruffles may be a little different—but I did want you to see the process I used. Try it. The painting is not difficult, and with patience and a good road map you can get there.

Mix your own black paint for the background. Mix enough black for several layers. Use a palette knife so the paint is dry; water will dilute it and produce gray.

Mix mostly Antwerp Blue with less Permanent Rose and even less New Gamboge. If it looks green, add the complement of green which is red. If it looks too blue, add more of the red and yellow. Keep altering the mix until you get a neutral black. It will work!

Mix a large enough amount so you can paint three layers. Try not to remix, because the blacks will not be the same. I usually use a small container with a lid. A film container will do. Mix the color on the palette, then place it in the container. Label it with the painting title.

When I have a black background, I usually select a mat that is a medium value. White is usually too much contrast. Remember that you should not see the mat before you see the painting. The artwork should draw your attention. The mat should support it but never become more important than the art.

Supplies

Winsor & Newton Watercolors: Permanent Rose, New Gamboge, Antwerp Blue, Magenta, Burnt Sienna, Winsor Emerald, Winsor Violet and Winsor Blue.

1 Paint the wet stage with New Gamboge, Winsor Emerald, Permanent Rose and a blue mix of Antwerp Blue + Permanent Rose. Use touches of New Gamboge on the upper right iris and buds. Use tints of Permanent Rose mainly on flowers; leave some areas white. Use the blue mix and green on leaf areas. Allow these to bleed and run. Soften the edges of color with a thirsty brush. Begin creating the folds and ruffles on the flowers.

Dry your paper and apply a layer of black in the background. (This will be done at least one more time for maximum coverage.)

To apply the mixed black paint (see chapter one for mixing instructions), wet the round brush and remove half of the water. Start close to an object and move around the design by continuously painting from the wet edge. This will help prevent overlap lines.

2 Paint an orange mix of Permanent Rose + New Gamboge on the inner areas of the beards. Pull out with water at the outer edges.

Use a mix that resembles Yellow Ochre (dull yellow) on both buds. The mix is New Gamboge + Permanent Rose + Antwerp Blue. As the wet area loses its shine, add small shapes of a brownish mix of these same three colors plus, on occasion, add in orange. You are just suggesting the way the foliage dries out and becomes similar to parchment as the bud develops into a flower.

Begin the flowers by painting the lightest values. There is not much white left on these. The dark shadows will create the illusion of more light. Begin the flower to the right by forming it with Magenta. The lower flower is Magenta and a cool blue-violet mix of Antwerp Blue + Permanent Rose. Use the same colors on the upper left iris with more use of the cooler mix.

Deepen the leaves to a middle value with blues and violets if they are lighter than the flowers.

Paint a wash on the stem. Paint Winsor Emerald on the left and New Gamboge on the right. Paint a second layer to all petals creating the folds. The two flowers on the left have mostly cools (Antwerp Blue + Permanent Rose mixed to a blue-violet) and a little warm (Permanent Magenta). The flower on the right is mostly warm and a little cool.

Wet one petal at a time. Paint in color to form ruffles. Soften the edges of the ruffles, parchment and stem areas with a damp brush and clean water.

Paint the green shading on the parchment area on the left side with Antwerp Blue + Burnt Sienna mixed to a blue-green. Streak it on and soften the edge toward the center. Paint the leaves by chiseling on the color and soften with a damp brush.

3 Soften the flower edges that appear hard with clean water. Paint the strongest darks—the dark, rich shadows created from the backlighting—in the dark purple crevices of the flowers. Use Winsor Violet + Winsor Blue. Blend out the edge. Repeat this process if the first layer is not dark enough.

Create the look of ridges on the leaves by adding darker values and lifting light streaks with a damp, flat brush—simply slide it along the chisel edge.

Paint a second layer of black in the background. If you need to touch up a few areas with a third layer, you may do so knowing that the premixed color will match. Your background should look vibrant and completely covered.

Chapter Five: Intermediate Projects

Supplies

Paper: 11½"×22"
(29.2cm×55.9cm) Winsor &
Newton 260-lb. cold-press.

**Winsor & Newton
Watercolors:** New Gamboge,
Yellow Ochre, Burnt Sienna,
Antwerp Blue, Cobalt Blue,
Winsor Blue, Permanent
Rose, Permanent Magenta,
Alizarin Crimson and Purple
Madder Alizarin.

This chapter includes a variety of flowers. The paintings range in size from 11"×15" (27.9cm×38.1cm) to
full size sheets of 22"×30" (55.9cm×76.2cm). The
"White Rose" and "Magnolias" are the full sheets.
When you have gained some confidence, do try the
larger format. Each painting may use a slightly different technique of blending or applying the paint. I hope
you will gain experience by painting them.

Lilies of Gold

These lilies create a pattern of overlapping, interlocking shapes. The high-contrast background defines them. Each petal is created by the application of several layers.

Paint New Gamboge on stamens and end shapes. Dry and then *mask off* the stamens. Paint on washes of Winsor Emerald on lower third of paper. The main color in this floral is a dull peach. It is made with New Gamboge, Permanent Rose and a touch of Antwerp Blue. It is warm and transparent, but not bright. The brightness in the painting comes from the yellow, the white paper and the small red-orange accents.

Paint color on background and leaves. Start at the top. Make this the darkest area. Use a large round brush and apply thick, juicy color. Use Winsor Blue, Permanent Magenta, a mix of Winsor Blue + Burnt Sienna, a mix of Antwerp Blue + Burnt Sienna.

The middle plane should be a middle value. Paint over the leaves with mostly cool blue-green mixes. The strong darks are painted in later. Use more water in your mixes to lighten them plus use some Yellow Ochre. The lower third gets a little lighter by using more yellow over some leaves. Dry this stage.

Paint darks between the leaves and petals with Winsor Blue and Magenta separately, allowing them to blend into each other. Then paint some areas by brushing the colors together. Occasionally use Winsor Blue and Purple Madder Alizarin. Most of your leaves will have some variety to them with this method. Soften

the edges of the leaves. You may prefer to work on the flowers for a while; however, I will complete the leaf instructions here so you may go back and forth. You may want to work on the flowers and, while waiting for them to dry, complete leaves.

Keep the leaves under the large lily the lightest. These have the most detail as well as the most value changes. The *ridges* on these were done by painting a dark value of Burnt Sienna and Antwerp Blue mixed until green. Apply this to part of the leaf and pull out the edge of the color with a damp brush. Allow a ridge to form. Leave one edge hard.

Some of the more distant leaves were wet and a darker blue-green mix applied by using the chisel of the brush. The more distant ones are simply leaf shapes with no detail. The shadows in the leaves are a thin veil of Antwerp Blue + New Gamboge.

Soften the edges of all lilies and buds. The petals that appear to be cooler are reflecting the sky color. The ones that are warmer and more yellow are capturing the sunlight. It may sometimes take two layers to achieve the strength of color you need. Simply dry each layer well before applying the next. The whitest areas of the petals are in direct sunlight. These were not masked off but were carefully painted around.

1 Paint New Gamboge on stamens and some lower leaves in the front. Paint on washes of Winsor Emerald as well. Paint the background using a large round brush and alternate values and colors. Mask over the stamens.

2 Paint the background shapes that are between the flower petals.

LILIES

Begin painting the cool petals on the largest flower. They are the ones on the right. Paint on a wash with a mix of Permanent Magenta + Cobalt Blue. Leave the white areas untouched. Paint this darker (use less water) to the back edge to create the illusion that the edge rolls back.

When this is *dry*, make a dull peach color with New Gamboge + Permanent Rose + a touch of Antwerp Blue. Paint this into the area closest to the stem, and pull it out about halfway up on the petal. This adds a little warmth.

When dry, add Purple Madder Alizarin to area closest to stem and pull out to create the darkest value on the flowers. When dry, add a layer of peach over all but the white areas. A final wash of New Gamboge + Permanent Rose will add brightness. The underside of the right petal, where it rolls under, is simply Purple Madder Alizarin + Cobalt Blue. When it is dry, paint on a cool shadow made with Antwerp Blue + Permanent Rose. Again you may choose to skip around and paint one layer on each petal. I will describe all the layers in each area so you will know where to locate them in your instructions. Remember to dry each layer before applying another.

Now paint the lighter petals on the left. Because this needs to stay light, it is best to wet the entire petal with clean water. Apply Yellow Ochre near the stem and blend outward to fade to the white paper. Apply a little at the outer edge and blend in. Dry this and apply a dull peach made with New Gamboge + Permanent Rose + Antwerp Blue. Dry the petal, then apply a small shape at the end with this mix in a smaller area near center and blend out. This will be your dark. The narrow white petal that bends has this mix painted on the underside as well as the side edge. The rest of the petal is left white.

There is a final warm shadow painted on the narrow petal with New Gamboge + Permanent Rose + a touch of Antwerp Blue (dull peach). The lower right

3 Begin defining the foreground leaves and painting the first layer on the flowers.

4 Deepen the flower layer to create form and depth. Complete the stamens.

petal is painted by wetting the petal, applying the Yellow Ochre and blending out halfway. Dry this and use the dull peach with more blue in it to cool it further. Create the center line by applying this near the stem area on the upper side of the vein line; blend out. Repeat this from the outside inward. Then apply the same mix to create the subtle ruffles on the outer edge. Soften the edges.

Final tint is a small accent of orange made with Permanent Rose + New Gamboge over the yellow closest to the front of the painting. The shadow is cool, thin Antwerp Blue and Permanent Rose.

Be mindful of the small dark separations between the petals. Keep them crisp. The shadows on the warm side of the flowers were painted first with the peach mix then accented with bright orange at the edges with New Gamboge + Permanent Rose.

The other petals and flowers are simply variations of these same types of layers. Use the final painting as reference and notice that the lower left has accents of orange made with Permanent Rose + New Gamboge. It has several white areas. The other flowers have less white left, even less orange and more Permanent Magenta. Sometimes use the Permanent Magenta alone and sometimes pick up a tad of Cobalt Blue with it.

5 Complete the other flowers by referring to the step-by-step instructions and the photo of the finished painting.

6 Paint the long buds and continue getting variety in the leaf shapes by using different values and mixes.

BUDS

Paint on a thin layer of Yellow Ochre or occasionally use New Gamboge. Dry. Paint a dull peach at the top next to this line and pull downward. Repeat at the bottom, applying paint and pulling upward. Keep the right side of each bud with less peach on it and use more on the final left shape. This will help contour it.

After the flowers are complete, remove the masking fluid. Paint orange down the left side of the long sta-

mens and the down right sides of the oval shapes on the top. On the left or under side of this oval shape, paint a mix of Purple Madder Alizarin + Alizarin Crimson. This will be a darker mix. Check the yellows throughout. If there are none in any of the outer leaves, you may wish to lift a little green and add some small washes of New Gamboge. Check the value of the upper portion of the painting. If yours is not as dark, add more thick, juicy mixes.

Peonies

My peony bush provides me with many interesting flower shapes to paint. The small bush is abundant with huge flowers at the height of blooming season. My intent was to accent their size. With the goal of creating a strong dramatic painting for a relatively small area, I choose a high contrast.

Supplies

Winsor & Newton Watercolors: New Gamboge, Raw Sienna, Permanent Rose, Magenta, Antwerp Blue, Winsor Green, Winsor Violet, Burnt Sienna.

Paper: 11"×22" (27.9cm×55.9cm) Winsor & Newton 260-lb. Rough.

1 Worksheet—wet entire paper and paint the wet stage. Paint some yellow (New Gamboge) onto the flowers and some cool mix on the right petals. Use Cobalt Blue for the cool mix on the flowers and in the background. Paint small areas of Winsor Emerald to the background and leaf area. Allow some white to remain on the flowers, especially on the left side.

This shows a variety of ways to paint the petals. One column shows where to apply the color and the other shows it blended. You may prewet each petal or work dry.

2 Paint the dark background around the flowers. Refer to the Worksheet for a visual guide. Use a 1-inch flat brush and thick, juicy paint. Brush-mix Winsor Violet + Winsor Green. Each time you mix, try to get a variance in the color. You may get a blue, green and violet. Let the brushstrokes show. This will create a mottled effect. Go around all flowers and a few leaves. Soften the edges of the back flower petals and allow some of this background color to come into the edges.

3 The petals are painted in a variety of colors. Use Raw Sienna on the yellow ones. Use Cobalt Blue to create some cool petals to the right. Use Antwerp Blue + Permanent Rose mixed to a blue-violet for the deeper values on the cool sides.

4 Continue to develop more petals. When you want to roll a petal, you may apply the color in several layers. Paint the petals to the left—the warmer sides of the flowers—with Permanent Magenta. These were very opened, floppy petals without too many contours. It should be an easy way to paint the look of a complicated flower. You will get the illusion of the shape of the flower by creating a roundness with the overall ball shape rather than contouring each petal.

5 Paint a wash of New Gamboge on the buds. Dry this. Make a cool blue mix of Antwerp Blue + a little Permanent Rose. Paint this on the bud to create a layer of middle value. Paint it on in a *C* shape on the right side of the bud about a third of the way over, and blend this transition line with a brush that has 50 percent of the water out of it.

Dry this and repeat with another layer of the same mix only about one-fourth of the way over. Soften the light edges into the background. This should produce a ball effect.

6 Continue deepening the flower colors.

7 Paint on New Gamboge to the vein areas and the edges of a few leaves under the center flower. Paint in the green with a mix of Antwerp Blue + Burnt Sienna. Create a few more negative shapes of leaves by darkening the background with the original background mixes.

If you want a more realistic peony you may want to contour each petal with the layering technique. You may also want to detail all of the leaves. We have created the impression of the flowers.

Pink Dogwood

Dogwood can be interpreted in so many ways. This is
a rather up-close and personal look.

Supplies

*Winsor & Newton
Watercolors:* New Gamboge,
Alizarin Crimson, Permanent
Rose, Purple Madder Alizarin,
Winsor Emerald, Burnt
Sienna, Antwerp Blue.

Paper: 11″×15″
(27.9cm×38.1cm) Arches
300-lb. cold-press.

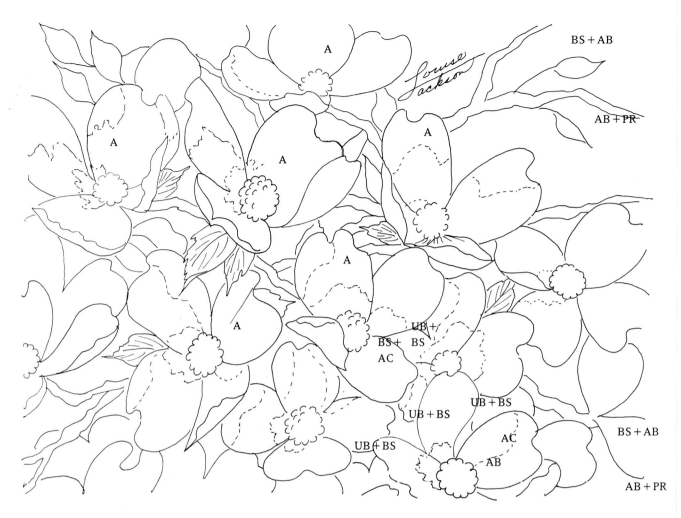

BS + AB

AB + PR

A

A

A

A

A

A

A

UB +
BS +
AC

BS

UB + BS

UB + BS

UB + BS

BS + AB

AC

AB

AB + PR

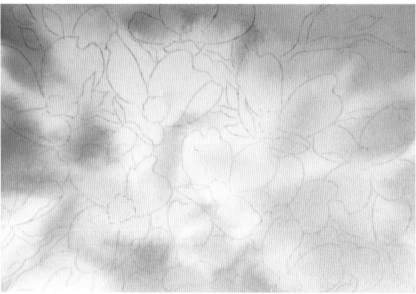

1 For the wet stage paint on Winsor Emerald, Purple Madder Alizarin and a blue mix of Antwerp Blue + Permanent Rose. Dry this completely.

2 Paint a thin wash of color over the outer flowers. Paint around the lighter flowers, blending this into the background. In the upper right corner, allow the background colors from the first stage to remain. It will help create a variety of color and value. Use a thin mix on the blue side of Antwerp Blue + Permanent Rose. Dry this.

3 Paint one more layer of the same mix around all of the flowers to define their shapes. Dry this and begin to paint in the darker blue mix in the background around the center flowers. Paint this mix in the background on a diagonal from the upper left side to the lower right. You may create a few more flower shapes as well.

There is one more strong, dark layer—use a mix of Antwerp Blue + Purple Madder Alizarin. This may be painted now or at the end.

Paint a wash of yellow-green on the two small leaves that appear the brightest. Use New Gamboge and a touch of Antwerp Blue. Paint a wash of green made with Antwerp Blue and Burnt Sienna to the rest. Paint the shadows on the dogwood petals with Purple Madder Alizarin + Alizarin Crimson (for the unpainted flowers) or Purple Madder Alizarin (for the cool ones).

4 Wet the flower centers with water, and dab in New Gamboge. Allow this to bleed into the water. The second flower is an illustration of the color placement. The third flower shows you what the effect will be when the petals are wet first and have color applied then directed with a thirsty brush. Use Purple Madder Alizarin for this. On the lightest petals use Purple Madder Alizarin and Permanent Rose. Each petal is painted in this manner.

When they are complete, refer to the lower right illustration to see how the strong, dark red is applied to the main flowers. This is a thick, juicy mix of Alizarin Crimson and Purple Madder Alizarin. Paint it on dry paper and use a round brush with half of the water removed to pull out the transition line.

The center gets a *c* shaped layer of Burnt Sienna on the left to create form. When dry, use a mix of Burnt Sienna + Alizarin Crimson to form the small *c* shapes. Corner load a no. 10 flat brush and work on dry paper.

5 This is a close-up of some of the flowers. Paint in the branches with a wash of a dull brown. Mix this with Antwerp Blue + Permanent Rose + New Gamboge. Add in darks with a thicker mix of the same and some tints of Purple Madder Alizarin. Refer back to Step Four for the placement.

6 With a light wash of brown, paint a branch in the empty space of the background. Add a few small leaves. Keep strengthening the red—it may take several layers. Add a few cool shadows on some flowers with a mix of Antwerp Blue + Permanent Rose.

7 Paint the strongest darks in the background with Antwerp Blue + Purple Madder Alizarin. Paint the leaves with a mix of Antwerp Blue and Burnt Sienna. To create a little texture to the tiny shapes, simply paint the shapes around the yellow and leave it unblended.

White Poinsettias

Supplies

Winsor & Newton Watercolors: Winsor Emerald, Permanent Rose, Antwerp Blue, Cobalt Blue, Burnt Sienna, Purple Madder Alizarin.

Brushes: 1- and 2-inch as well as no. 10 and no. 20 flat, no. 8 round.

Derwent Pencils: no. 34 Golden Brown [dull yellow], no. 10 Madder Carmine [deep red], no. 35 Copper Beech [brown].

The freshness and interesting shapes of the poinsettias add to the beauty of the holiday season. I love to hang paintings that are suitable for the season. In our home we try to hang winter flower paintings for the holidays.

Make this simpler by using colored pencils. Using them first before any water is added will save lots of detail work later and make it easy to keep the berries round. After the water is applied, simply ignore the yellow pencil lines and let them show or disappear.

Use yellow to draw in growth lines to many but not all of the white petal shapes. Add red to the edges of some petals. Circle the berries with red. Use the brown on the holly branches. Draw down the left side and color in the right half. This will leave a light area when it is wet. Originally I put green on some leaves and it disappeared, so there is no reason for you to use the green.

1 Mask off the holly berries and the centers of the flowers. In the poinsettias, the "berries" in the center are the actual flower and the rest are leaves that change color. For our purposes, we will refer to the poinsettias' leaves as flower petals. Also, mask the tiny connecting stems to the top petals in the flowers, near the center. We will refer to this area as the connecting stems.

2 After the wet stage, if you find the yellow pencil lines have really faded, simply dry the paper and draw the lines again with pencil lightly. I prefer to do them twice rather than draw so heavily that it dents the paper. Wet the paper thoroughly and apply both Permanent Rose and Winsor Emerald separately up near the flower and a blue mix of Antwerp Blue + Permanent Rose mixed to a mid-value through the rest of the background. Notice that the flower on the right has a lot of cool color on it. This area will recede the most. Sprinkle salt just to create some interest.

Dry the paper and paint the blue mix in the center areas of the flowers, between the connecting stems as well as the center of the painting where the flowers meet. Reinforce the pencil on the right side of the branches.

3 Make a blue mix of Antwerp Blue + Permanent Rose. Side load the 2-inch brush with this mix and paint around the outside of the large petals. Walk the brush out on occasion to avoid an outlined look.

Paint another layer to attach the connecting stems in the center of the flowers to the petals underneath.

Put water on the holly branches and direct the brown color inward. Paint a few flower leaves on the right side with thin green with a mix of Antwerp Blue + Burnt Sienna. Use the chisel edge of a no. 10 flat, damp brush to lift the growth lines.

Paint the holly leaves with the same color mix. Vary the value by using more water in the light ones, less in the dark ones. Lift the vein lines with a damp no. 10 flat.

4 Now make the flowers grow. Paint more negative background around some larger leaves. Think of it as carving leaf shapes out of the background. This will allow them to recede nicely. You may paint this with the large brush or the round. Use what works best for you.

When you paint the shape around the leaf, simply blend the color into the background. There are a few positive leaves that I painted on the left side of the upper flower.

5 Paint some tiny dark shapes in between the stems and a few between the flowers. This will give you a value guide. It helps me see that I need a lot more middle value. It also reminds me to save the lightest values on the left side of the flowers.

Remove the masking fluid that is on the berries. With your red pencil, draw around the highlight in each berry and fill in the berry. Take the tip of your round brush and carefully wet the berry so it appears smoother. Add some Purple Madder Alizarin to the right side of the circles to separate them.

If you are not using pencils at all you may, of course, do this with a brush. If you use paint, use Cadmium Red Medium (or Deep) for the first color. Then use the Purple Madder Alizarin.

6 Wet your branch and apply Purple Madder Alizarin to the right side. Direct the paint so it appears ragged (not smooth) of the left side of the branch. Begin to apply some of the red to the flower.

Even though these flowers are white, they need some color to create the form of each petal. Because I am imagining that the light source is from the left, I will try to keep that side warmer and a little brighter by using Permanent Rose on that side of the petals. Use Purple Madder Alizarin to the right side. Occasionally use Cobalt Blue as a bright accent. Use the blue mix of Antwerp Blue + Permanent Rose for all of the other cool petals.

Use a no. 20 flat and side load a damp brush to apply the paint. Set the color down, lift the brush to skip a small vein line, then set the brush down for the next stroke. Begin to paint some shadows at this time also. Use Purple Madder Alizarin on some. And a cool mix of Permanent Rose + Antwerp Blue on other shadow areas.

7 Each petal is treated a little differently to add interest to the overall flower. Rather than photorealism, remember that you are creating the illusion of a white flower. To add life to the flower we are using color rather than grays to create the form. Some of the petals in the strong light will have no paint on them or simply enough to turn the edge back.

Paint the shadows on the green petals with Antwerp Blue and Burnt Sienna and the ones on the white petals with Antwerp Blue and Permanent Rose. Paint in a couple of middle, dark areas to the background. Use thick, juicy Antwerp Blue + Purple Madder Alizarin and come out of it with a little green mix.

8 Side load a blue mix of Antwerp Blue + Permanent Rose to the upper right petals. To get this side of the flowers to recede, you want to make the outside similar in value and temperature.

At this point I decided to add more holly. I will add even more (shown on the drawing). Paint it in the same manner as the other leaves. Some will be painted over the background.

Paint the holly leaves with a wash of the green mix and add dark into the vein area. Paint a couple leaves on the right, darker to break up the value along the outside edge. On the darker ones, you may lift out some veins with a damp no. 10 flat brush.

Paint a thin wash of Antwerp Blue + Permanent Rose mixed to a blue, creating some negative space around some leaf shapes. Paint this around the lower portion, up the right side and over the top of the right side of your paper. Do the holly berries and stem the same as in Step five. Don't use the Purple Madder Alizarin on the very top berries—they will remain quieter with less value change.

9 Paint in more holly leaves and a few more berries. Vary the leaf mix with the amount of water you use. Finish the shading on the light flower petals. Use some Cobalt Blue as a cool on some petals for a brighter accent blue. Paint a blue wash over the top and down the right side of the top two flowers.

Go over the extreme darks with another layer of Antwerp Blue and Purple Madder Alizarin. Balance the darks by painting some small dark holly leaves throughout. Wash a few outer petals on the flowers with a wash of green mix made with Antwerp Blue plus Burnt Sienna. Check the shadows and reinforce them with another layer if they appear faded.

Amaryllis

These are large, stately flowers that grow on a stalk, but the grain of the flowers interested me. I used a *rake* brush to paint the grain or growth lines. You may also create them with a pointed round brush using many strokes.

This is a direct painting as well as a layering process. The background leaves are painted with layers of negative shapes painted around them. Each layer is dried, and each successive one changes value or temperature all the way to the black shapes.

Supplies

Paper: 18″ × 22″ (45.7cm × 55.9cm) Winsor & Newton rough 260-lb. cold-press.

Winsor & Newton Watercolors: New Gamboge, Permanent Rose, Antwerp Blue, Burnt Sienna, Purple Madder Alizarin, Winsor Red, Winsor Green, Ultramarine Blue and Alizarin Crimson.

Brush: ½-inch rake brush.

FLOWERS

Mask off stamens.

Paint in the yellow-green area first. Paint on New Gamboge, add yellow-green in the deep area with a mix of Antwerp Blue + New Gamboge.

The red of the flowers is a mix of Alizarin Crimson + Winsor Red. Each petal needs to be wet. Wet one petal, paint it and skip the ones next to it, leaving dry petals on either side. Allow the water to soak in and begin to lose its shine. Stroke on color with the rake brush. Follow the growth lines. Refer to direction of each petal. Direct and streak through any blooms or blossoms with the chisel edge of your thirsty no. 20 flat. Direct the streaks and see that the edges inside fade to white. Most of the color comes from the outside edge of the petal inward.

BACKGROUND

The lower half of the painting was done with medium to medium-dark values. Use the largest round brush you have. Each time you fill your brush, switch colors and allow them to merge. Work each color into the wet edge.

The top half of the background is a little lighter. Use the 2-inch flat to apply the first layer. Use a blue mix made with Antwerp Blue + Permanent Rose. Paint a layer over the upper left flower in the left corner. This will help it recede. Paint the stems with New Gamboge + Antwerp Blue. You may wet this area of the paper first, or paint on dry paper.

FLOWER CENTERS

Deepen the dark area with a black green mix of Alizarin Crimson + Winsor Green. To get your mix dark enough, use very little water. Strengthen reds with another layer of the red mix. Then deepen the edges that you want to recede the most with Purple Madder Alizarin using the rake brush on damp paper, or applying paint dry and directing the edges of the paint with a damp brush.

STEM

Paint dark down the left side with a dark mix to a green made with Antwerp Blue + Burnt Sienna.

Paint a line of yellow green (New Gamboge + a touch of Antwerp Blue) to the areas of the flower pet-

als that roll back from the center. Blend the transition line out. This is a reflected light.

BACKGROUND

Paint a thin layer of green with Antwerp Blue + Burnt Sienna around some leaves. Create the leaf shapes as you go. Be creative. It is not important to have them in the same place as mine. Simply create different shapes going in different directions. Dry this layer and paint on another layer. Use blue with a mix of Antwerp Blue + Permanent Rose. Use Winsor Green + Alizarin Crimson mixed to a black to paint in the strongest darks. Begin near the stem. Make each shape different. Add a little water to the mix to make some shapes of dark green as well as black.

The stamen area needs shadows. Paint below the masking fluid. Use a mix of transparent dull green. Make a mix of Antwerp Blue + New Gamboge + Permanent Rose. Paint this on as if you were painting shadows from the ovals on the tip of the stamen with this mix. Refer to the photo.

The main flower has a very long stamen that turns up. Try to keep the top of this white by painting a thin yellow-green wash on the white of the petal around the center. Dry the area.

STAMENS

Remove masking. Use a scrubby brush to soften the edges. Apply yellow-green on the stamens closest to the center. Pull out with New Gamboge on the brush so part of the stamen is yellow and part is white. Paint the green shadow color down the right side of the turned-up stamen. This should give a roundness to it.

Any step that has been painted needs to be repainted as many times as it takes you to get the appropriate value. Shadows are painted with a dull gray-green from a mix of Antwerp Blue + Permanent Rose + New Gamboge. Make a darker mix of this to paint on the stem and leaves. Recede the leaves above the flowers with a thin blue wash of Antwerp Blue + Permanent Rose. Use a very thin wash of this on some of the outer flower petals to recede them.

Live with it a few days and keep pushing anything back that should recede more. This is the fun part of the layering process. Remember to always have the surface dry before adding another layer.

The background is painted in a direct manner using a large round brush. Paint the values darker on the lower portion and lighter above the flowers. Refer to notes on background and on the drawing for specific colors and techniques. The flower colors are painted to show the growth lines of the petals. Wet each petal and paint in color with a rake brush.

Paint the center green area of the flower by painting the yellow from the inside out. Charge in the yellow-green mix on the inner half. Paint the stamen ends when the flowers are painted.

The flower petals in the background have a layer of background color over them. This will help them recede. They need to have growth lines painted on them as well. Treat them the same as the lighter flowers.

Paint a layer of dark near the focal flowers in the background. This is the negative space painting that will add your strongest darks. It also gives you the opportunity to create some leaf shapes from the first background layer. Begin creating background leaves using thinner paint.

Strengthen the red on the flowers by repeating the first layer with the rake brush. This time use a thicker layer of paint.

Continue creating more leaves in the background by painting the space around them. Dry each layer before proceeding with the next.

Paint transparent shadows cast from the stamens and the petals.

Check the values against the finished photo of my painting.

1 Background color was applied to dry paper. Each stroke overlaps the next one. Use a large 1-inch flat brush and work in one continuous direction. Each time you apply a color, let it touch into the wet edge of the previous stroke. Use a combination of these colors: Winsor Emerald + Cobalt Blue + French Ultramarine Blue + Winsor Violet. They will be a medium value. Begin to model the rose by wetting the right outer petals and painting on a cool blue mix of Antwerp Blue + a little Permanent Rose. On the left side, wet one or two petals at a time and paint on a warm mix of Antwerp Blue + more Permanent Rose. Occasionally add a little of the cool mix to this side.

2 Model the form of the petal. Wet each petal and paint only as large a section as you can blend at that time. Blend the transition line out in the large areas with a damp, thirsty brush, a no. 20 flat or a 1-inch flat. To create the large, deep inner bowl area on the right side of the rose, you may have to do several layers of this. Allow each layer to completely dry before applying another. Keep your water very clean because even the tiniest bit of color in your blending water will deposit a color line on your white rose.

3 Begin to develop your background by painting some negative space around the leaves. Create the leaf forms by putting a value of color around them. You may have more or less than mine and that would work in the painting.

4 The leaves on the right side have a lot of detail. Use Antwerp Blue + Burnt Sienna mixed to a green, as well as Winsor Green and Winsor Violet for a dark cool mix. You may also use Alizarin Crimson + Burnt Sienna for some of the central veins. Paint the dark area on the lower right side of background with a mix of Winsor Green + Alizarin Crimson to a very dark green. When this is dry, you may want to carve out a few very dark leaf shapes by painting black around this dark value.

At this point, make a mix of black (approximately a tablespoonful). Use a palette knife and mostly Antwerp Blue + a little less Permanent Rose + a very little New Gamboge. This should give you a clean, transparent, vibrant black. Put this in a container with a lid so you will have the same mix for a second coat. Paint a layer of Antwerp Blue + Burnt Sienna on any leaves that are not dark enough. They need to be dark enough to recede into the black background before painting detail work on them.

5 The last step is to paint your black background. You may choose to carve out a few more dark green leaves when you are doing it. Start at the point where the rose petal touches the bottom of the paper and work away from that. Always try to work into the wet edge of the color. Use this black to clean up edges on the rose petal and to create ragged edges on the leaves. Use only as much water as is needed to make the paint flow. I use a large round for this.

Continue around the rose until the first layer is complete. Dry this completely. Repeat with a second layer. Do a third layer if necessary. If you have any thin areas, you may want to add another layer to those areas. This is why it is important to have the black mix already made.

The water drops on the rose are simply shadowed underneath with the same cool mix used on the petals. Use the same mix to create the upper shape of the water drops, and scrape out your highlights with a craft knife

For the shadows, paint a wash of the cool mix. Use enough water so this is just a thin veil of color. Take your round brush with most of the water out and touch into the edge of the shadow line. This will soften it slightly without moving it anywhere.

Wet the background around the rose. Paint with a large flat brush. Even though most of the background is black, this stage will create a few values we will use, and it will tone the white paper and allow you to judge the rose values better. Begin creating the form of each petal with warm and cool colors.

Define a few edges of the rose by placing some darks in the background.

The strongest dark area of the rose is painted and blended to fade out. Begin to create the leaf shape by painting a strong dark in the background.

Create the leaf shapes with careful attention to the jagged edges by painting them dark.

Continue developing the petal form using as many layers as it takes to make them lift, roll and recede. Waterdrops can be added.

Paint the colors on the leaves. Give them a lot of detail, especially on the right side. Paint on the first layer of blue black. When you paint the second layer, you may create a few leaf shapes by painting the space around them. The black will need to be painted at least twice, depending on how thick you apply your paint. Three times is pretty normal for most people. Be sure you mix enough of the color beforehand. This is the finished painting.

Magnolias

The magnolias of the south are wonderful subjects. The foliage is rich and dark. The flowers are powerful and stately. The shapes and contours are as individual as a rose. This composition was created from a compilation of several photos taken during a visit to New Orleans.

This is a large painting and includes several different techniques. Before you begin, please re-read chapter two and practice these techniques.

Begin painting in the lower right corner. This will allow you to improve as you go, and by the time you are ready to work on the focal area, you will be comfortable with the blending.

To paint the background, use a large round brush with juicy mixes of Winsor Violet and Winsor Green. Sometimes lean this to the blue and alternately lean it to the green and to the violet. Don't allow it to be too bright green or violet. In smaller amounts you may use a little Raw Sienna as well as some Burnt Sienna. This is predominately cool painting and needs some small warm areas.

This line indicates a cup form.

Find a stopping point before you paint all the way up the side. If you imagine the side of a leaf shape, this will give you a place to rest. Even if you decide later not to have a leaf there, it will work into the background.

Each petal in this painting has a warm or cool look. The warm tones are mixed with transparent main three: New Gamboge + Permanent Rose + Antwerp Blue. Mix until it appears dull yellow, not as light or bright as Yellow Ochre. Each time you mix it, the color will vary. That adds interest, so don't try to duplicate your mix each time. I will refer to this as your warm flower mix. The cool flower mix is on the blue-grey side. Make it with Cobalt Blue + Permanent Rose + a tiny amount of New Gamboge.

Supplies

Paper: 22″×30″ (55.9cm×76.2cm) Arches 300-lb. cold press.

Winsor & Newton Watercolors: New Gamboge, Yellow Ochre, Raw Sienna, Burnt Sienna, Cobalt Blue, Antwerp Blue, Ultramarine Blue, Permanent Rose, Winsor Green, Winsor Violet.

1 Wet one petal at a time with water. Apply color and blend. Use your no. 8 round to apply paint to the area to be shaded. Then you have a choice blending the transition line. For the most part, I chose to use a no. 20 flat that had about 50 or 60 percent of the water out. Occasionally, try to use the damp round brush in a pull-blending manner as described in the blending worksheet (on pages 23-24).

Apply your warm tones to the petals behind the center with the warm flower mix. Blend each color line before the paper dries. The other petals on this flower are painted with your cool flower tones. Dry the petals and begin to apply some dark values to the background. Use a large round brush and juicy paint. Allow it to appear mottled and unblended.

There are two types of texture in the magnolia center. The upper portion can be best described as dabs of color. With the end of the round brush, dab on New Gamboge, leaving holes. Dab on Yellow Ochre in between, leaving some white. On the right side dab on a green mixed with Antwerp Blue + Burnt Sienna. This should create some contour. They will run and bleed together.

The bottom portion needs to have contour as well. Layer the warm flower mix overall, then shade down the left side with Burnt Sienna. When this is dry, use the tip of the round or a liner brush to paint on what appears as little hairs with thin Burnt Sienna.

Paint a wash of Yellow Ochre on the long leaf coming through the flower. Dry. Paint the top half warm with Burnt Sienna + a touch of Antwerp Blue. Paint the bottom green with Antwerp Blue + Burnt Sienna mixed to a green.

2 Paint a wash of Antwerp Blue + Permanent Rose + New Gamboge mixed to a blue on the flower that is above the first. This will make it recede even before you begin to shade it. Paint this wash on the leaves to the left as well.

The branches are painted as the background colors are applied. Make a brown mix with Ultramarine Blue + Burnt Sienna. Use a round brush to apply this mix to the top edge of a branch. Quickly clean and remove half the water from your brush and blend the transition line. Allow this to dry and repeat the same process on the other side. If you are new to this type of blending, I suggest that you apply only about 1″ of paint, then blend it. The branches should look rough.

Begin to create leaves by painting in some dark shapes around them (refer to the negative space exercise on pages 15-16). Use a dark mix of Winsor Violet + Winsor Green mixed again to a variety of colors. Use a very dark green with a 1-inch flat brush to paint on the shape.

On some of the leaf shapes you may use your green mix of Antwerp Blue + Burnt Sienna. You may lift out color to create leaf shapes as well. Use your no. 20 flat and a damp brush to lift out the lights and the veins. Allow each leaf to dry before you lift. If you have not done this before, refer to the leaf technique worksheet in chapter three to learn how.

3 Begin to shade your blue flower the same as in no. 1. This time use a cool mix of Antwerp Blue + Permanent Rose + New Gamboge simply because it will get a little darker with the Antwerp Blue instead of the Cobalt Blue. Paint the little shapes near the center with a mix of Raw Sienna + Permanent Rose.

4 Fill in the background as you paint each flower. Do not be a slave to my composition on the leaves. If it works better to place more or fewer leaves, or use some different shapes, please feel free to do so. Add in a little Raw Sienna to add warmth on occasion. It is important to soften the edges of the flowers at some point. Some artists prefer to do this as they paint each section, while others prefer to soften at completion. Just don't forget this step.

5 Now work on the upper right flower. To increase the variety of color in the other flowers, continue to use the yellow mix, and on occasion use the Yellow Ochre as well as Raw Sienna. Alternately use the blue mix of Antwerp Blue + Permanent Rose + New Gamboge as well as the mix made with Cobalt Blue.

Base the tall narrow leaf coming through the upper right flower with Yellow Ochre. Allow to dry. Do the shading with Raw Sienna, and deepen with the warm flower mix. For the lower triangle of warm dark in the front petal, use the flower mix from no. 1 with a little more red. The darker areas in the cool petals are the cool mix with less water.

This flower's center is simpler and less is showing. Dab on New Gamboge as well as Yellow Ochre. Shade with a reddish version of the flower mix. Add more dark positive leaves and branches.

6 For the large magnolia in the center, it will be easier to mask off the center and the long stamens before painting the petals. When this is dry, paint the background in that area with a very dark mix of Winsor Violet + Winsor Green mixed to a blue. This will add a strong contrast to the area.

Paint on a wash of New Gamboge to upper portion. Dab on Raw Sienna. Paint little hair-like lines with thin Burnt Sienna. The long lines on the right are heavier lines of Burnt Sienna. The very dark brown at the bottom is Ultramarine Blue + Burnt Sienna.

7 Large magnolia—Repeat the use of the color previously used. Add some reddish mix by adding more red to the flower mix. Remember, as you layer and want darker values, use less water in your mixes. How many layers does it take? That depends on the amount of color and the amount of water you use.

To keep the flower white and clean, it is best to proceed slowly. This is your focal flower so make it the most interesting. Surround it with the most dark and have the most value changes in it.

8 There are a few pieces of stamens that fall into the petals. Paint them with Yellow Ochre and deepen with Burnt Sienna.

When the background is covered and dried, add many large dark leaf shapes. When you need a break from working on the flowers, do some lifting on the leaves.

9 The upper left flower is partially closed. However, the petals are painted the same way. There are some on the left that are beginning to age, so they are based with the yellow flower mix and shaded with a deeper value. The petals have some interesting shadows on them, so simply paint the cool shapes as you see them.

Notice the light leaf under the flower and the twisted ones to the right. Again, this adds more interest in the upper left quarter of the paper.

10 When you have completed the flowers, paint the shadows. They are transparent, so mix them from New Gamboge + Antwerp Blue + Permanent Rose. Mix the color so it is a dull version of the object that the shadow falls on. Don't make them simply gray as they can be boring.

Before you frame your painting, live with it a day or two. Check the values of things. You may continue to correct and alter anything.

centers with New Gamboge. Shade or dot with Purple Madder Alizarin. We will return to these later. Add leaves as you go with the Burnt Sienna + Antwerp Blue mix. You may also make a darker green mix with Winsor Green + Alizarin Crimson. Use this in leaves that are closer to the design and near the roses.

For the four petal flowers on the upper left corner, base each petal with thin Permanent Rose, and shade with Purple Madder Alizarin + Alizarin Crimson. Add New Gamboge for center and a few dots near the center of Purple Madder Alizarin. These should stay quiet due to their position in the painting.

Step 5. The strong color of the purple wild iris to the left of the top rose adds interest in this area. Paint the shape with Winsor Violet. The center light area was painted with Permanent Rose, and the Winsor Violet was painted into it. Add a little New Gamboge for the beards. Surround this flower with a few very dark leaves. Develop a few strong dark areas close to the ribbon and the roses. Use a mix of Antwerp Blue + Purple Madder Alizarin.

Paint in the cool leaves at upper left. They are simple leaf shapes painted with a thin mix of Antwerp Blue + Purple Madder Alizarin.

Finish the top zinnia by painting short overstrokes of Winsor Violet for the top petals. On the lower zinnia paint in the darks to separate the petals with Purple Madder Alizarin. Side load them in if you are able.

The long stamens in the larger flower are painted with a mix of Winsor Violet + Purple Madder Alizarin.

The roses are each painted the same way. My goal was to keep them simple and create the appearance that some petals were lost into the next one. Therefore, each petal was not separated and rolled.

Paint the red first. Refer to the finished photo for this. Use a mix of Winsor Red + Alizarin Crimson. I wanted to have this a little brighter red. Because the warmer red is in the focal area, it still allows the overall painting to remain cool. Paint in some New Gamboge to the yellow or warm-looking petals. Keep this very pale.

Soften the outside edges of the rose with a damp brush. Then for a duller yellow, mix New Gamboge with a little Winsor Violet, and use this to separate some petals mostly on the right side. Separate the cooler-looking petals with thin blue-grey made with Antwerp Blue + Permanent Rose + a little New Gamboge. On occasion, I used a red mix at the outer edge of a petal. Leave some of the light petals with no paint on them at all. Paint on a few shadows with a thin mix of Antwerp Blue + Permanent Rose mixed to a blue.

Illustration 1 shows the Purple Madder Alizarin base color painted on the burgundy Zinnia. Paint New Gamboge in the center. (For detail, refer to the bottom of illustration 3.

Illustration 2 shows the lighter, upper zinnia based with Permanent Magenta. Paint New Gamboge in the center. When this is dry, you may paint short overstroke petals of juicy Winsor Violet.

In illustration 3, achieve this detail by side loading a flat brush with Purple Madder Alizarin and painting around petal shapes.

Illustrations 4 and 5 show that these petals are based with Permanent Rose, and the blue mix of Antwerp Blue + Permanent Rose is applied to the outer edge and near the center of each petal while the Permanent Rose is wet. Paint New Gamboge to the very center.

Illustration 6 shows you some very simple leaf shapes, which is mostly what I used.

Illustration 7 shows the upper left small flowers. The lower left petal shows color placement. Wet each petal first. Paint on Purple Madder Alizarin and direct it with a thirsty brush. Paint New Gamboge to the center to complete them.

Illustration 8 shows color placement and blending for the blush inside the roses.

Illustration 9 shows color placement for the bow.

Illustration 10 shows the leaves in the upper left corner. Base with a mix of Purple Madder Alizarin + Antwerp Blue to a dull blue. With a damp brush, lift out streaks.

Illustration 11 shows the tiny pink flowers above the top rose. They are a little different. The one on the left shows the color placement for Permanent Rose. Try to leave little dry areas as you apply water from the center out. Then apply the Permanent Rose at the outer edges and New Gamboge in the center. As it dries, add a few dots of Purple Madder Alizarin under the center.

Illustration 12 shows the stamens painted with Purple Madder Alizarin after the flowers are dry.

1 This illustration shows several steps. Start with the bow. To suggest lace in a very simple manner, you may use a piece of lace or a paper doily. If you prefer, you may paint in some tiny dark shapes (the holes in the lace). Paint water around the roses and ribbons and apply the colors for the wet stage.

2 This is the first stage on all of the flowers. Refer to the step-by-step text as well as the flower worksheet. You may begin adding in the strong darks with a dark green mix of Winsor Green + Alizarin Crimson as well as Antwerp Blue + Purple Madder Alizarin. Use this for some darker leaves. Paint the lighter small leaf shapes with Burnt Sienna + Antwerp Blue. Paint the upper left long ones with a thin, blue mix of Antwerp Blue + Purple Madder Alizarin. Lift out streaks.

3 Develop the rose. Soften the outside edges with a damp brush. The red mix of Winsor Red + Alizarin Crimson adds a warm accent. Refer to illustration eight on the worksheet. The top illustration shows the color placement and the lower one shows how it should look blended. Use a round brush with 50 percent of the water removed and pull out the color. The temperature change of the red, yellow and blue creates the variety. The purple flower adds life to the area.

4 The zinnia centers have Alizarin Crimson side loaded to the left side. The lower one has an oval of dots added to the center.

A wash was added to the background, near the bow to create a soft, mid-value area. It is important to paint strong dark areas around the roses to make them appear light. Remember that without those darks the roses won't look white. The darkest and brightest colors are placed closest to the focal area—the roses.

Vase Study

This exercise will help in painting the *Cobalt Vase With Lilacs* (on pages 103-108). It may also be a vase you might choose with another flower arrangement.

Trace one vase onto your paper. There are four layers. Dry each one thoroughly before applying the next. Refer to the illustrations on the drawing, below, to see the color placement.

Supplies

Winsor & Newton Watercolors: French Ultramarine Blue, Winsor Violet, Permanent Rose.

Brushes: no. 8 round, no. 10 flat, small scrubby brush.

Other Supplies: Art Masking Fluid.

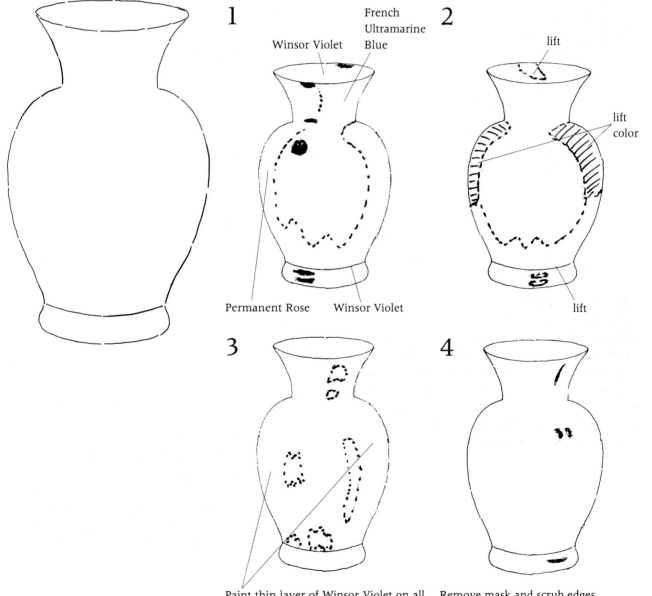

1
Winsor Violet
French Ultramarine Blue
Permanent Rose
Winsor Violet

2
lift
lift color
lift

3
Paint thin layer of Winsor Violet on all but inside dotted areas.

4
Remove mask and scrub edges.

1 (Top left) Mask off the small dark shapes on the drawing. Paint the inner top area and the bottom rim with Winsor Violet. Begin at the top right edge of the front of the vase. Paint on thick and juicy French Ultramarine Blue. Charge in Permanent Rose to the outside edge in the dotted line area. Aim the brush toward the edge to keep the outside edge neat.

2 (Top right) Take a damp brush and lift off a little color in the dotted line shapes. This will create some lighter areas.

3 (Bottom left) Paint a thin layer of Ultramarine Blue over the violet areas both on the top and bottom. Lift the paint on the front edge. Paint a thin layer of Winsor Violet to the areas outside the dotted lines. This will allow that blue to appear more transparent and brilliant. This is what gives the illusion of cobalt glass.

4 (Bottom right) Remove the masking fluid. Scrub the edges. Allow the color to work in to the white areas. Lift out a few more places to create some small lights bouncing around.

Cobalt Vase With Lilacs

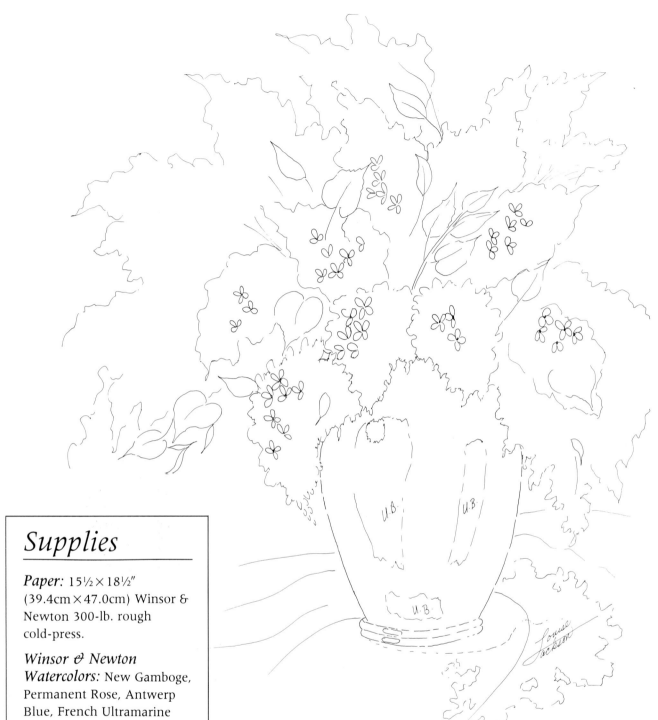

Supplies

Paper: 15½ × 18½"
(39.4cm × 47.0cm) Winsor &
Newton 300-lb. rough
cold-press.

*Winsor & Newton
Watercolors:* New Gamboge,
Permanent Rose, Antwerp
Blue, French Ultramarine
Blue, Burnt Sienna, Winsor
Green, Winsor Violet. White
Gouache (optional).

Brushes: 2-inch flat, 1-inch
flat, no. 8 round, small
scrubby brush.

Other Supplies: Sheet of
acetate, craft knife or electric
stencil cutter, Art Masking
fluid, soap.

The focus of this painting is more on the vase than
the cluster flowers. The lilacs are meant to give the
impression of lilacs rather than realistic accuracy. Mask
off the highlights on the vase and lilacs. Use a round
brush and do small petal-shaped strokes on the left side
of three lilacs. Allow this to dry naturally.

1 This is the wet stage. Get the paper very wet. With the 1-inch brush, apply some gray to the outer top edges, moving inward. Mix Permanent Rose + (Antwerp Blue + New Gamboge for the gray. Then apply all other colors with a blue-violet (Antwerp Blue + Permanent Rose) and a red-violet (Permanent Rose + Antwerp Blue). Use them alternately. Place more cool on the right side and warm on the left. Paint in long strokes of the same on the tablecloth, leaving some white.

Next, during the damp stage, use the 1-inch brush and pick up more pigment and less water. Imagine that you are creating the form of each lilac. Apply the darks to the right side of each cluster. Do this quickly, simply making brushstrokes. Hopefully your paper will still be damp enough for the next step to soften and bleed.

Take the round brush and apply small lilac-shaped petal strokes to the outside edges of each of these shapes. You must remove most of the water from the brush for this to work. Fill the brush, then lay it on your towels to pull the water out. If the brush drags, the paper has started drying. If so, try a wee bit more water. Dry the paper thoroughly.

2 Paint the first layer on the vase. Use the largest round brush you have. Aim the brush to the outside edges so you keep a very straight, neat edge on the container.

Begin on the left side and paint on dry paper. Paint in thick, juicy French Ultramarine Blue. Paint about half, then charge in Permanent Rose down the left side and across the bottom. Do not carry much water with this color.

Quickly resume the blue to complete the other side. Charge in Permanent Rose down the right side and across the bottom.

It is best not to touch it. Just let it dry as it is. Paint in some of this blue as petal strokes on the right side of some of the lilacs that are in front. Dry this stage.

3 Paint a red-violet layer with Winsor Violet on the bottom rim of the vase. Use a red-violet mix of Permanent Rose + Antwerp Blue on the lilacs with the masking on them. Let the existing color show. Simply make more little strokes. Dry and remove the masking fluid on the lilacs only.

4 With your red-violet mix, paint more small lilac petals over the edges of some of the white (so you don't have to soften the edges). Paint some dots of Winsor Violet into the center of some blossom clusters, even if they are not distinguishable.

Paint in some simple green leaves, using Winsor Green + Permanent Rose.

If your cluster of lilacs loses its cone form, you may use a stencil and scrub out some light areas; lift out petals with a damp brush; or, use white gouache. If you use white, mix it with a little color for a light value.

Next, check the drawing to see where the French Ultramarine Blue shapes are on the vase. Paint a juicy wash of Winsor Violet over all of the vase except these spaces. Paint over the bottom rim as well. Take a damp brush and lift out the reflecting shapes. They appear as a warm violet at both sides of the vase.

Paint another thin wash of blue over the blue shapes on the vase. Lift out two streaks on the right side of the bottom rim and paint blue.

Paint some larger leaf shapes in and over the edge of some lilacs. Use Antwerp Blue + Burnt Sienna mixed to a green, as well as Winsor Green + Permanent Rose for a few dark ones.

5 The first lilac shows the application of paint. The second shows what it looks like completed on white paper. You will already have some color under your flowers. Paint the color on, and quickly pick up clean water on your round brush. Remove a little water, then touch the edges of some of the color. This will allow some places to run and lighten, while some will remain a darker value.

The illustration on the right has a branch on it. On occasion, you may want one to show. You may also have partial branches as well as tiny connecting stems.

Upon completion of these steps, you may define some petal clusters by painting the negative shapes around them. This is purely a personal choice. Some people prefer to carry this through all of them. Some will be happy with just the cluster form. I usually fall somewhere in between. I like to paint a few areas of negative shapes just to suggest the blossoms and allow my viewer to know what they are. Do what pleases you.

Work from the front clusters to the back ones. Allow the receding ones to be more pale and less defined. Paint leaves as you proceed.

6 Paint the shadow shapes with Antwerp Blue + Permanent Rose. Complete the lilacs. Paint tiny dark shapes as negative space with dark mixes of Winsor Green + Permanent Rose, as well as Antwerp Blue + Permanent Rose around the lilacs.

Remove the masking fluid on the vase and scrub the edges. Allow the dark color to go into the edge. Add darks to some leaves and lift some veins.

To give the left side a little more life, wash a thin, splotchy Permanent Rose on some of the lilacs.

7 Rather than continue to darken the lilac shapes, I decided to cut a stencil and lighten some petals. If you have a craft knife to cut with, it will work. If you have an electric cutter, it is the easiest way to cut tiny petals. Cut seven or eight clusters out of acetate and lay this on a lilac. Use a wet toothbrush to scrub with. Pick up the acetate and blot the paper. The water will run under the stencil, but should not cause damage. When these are dry, repaint some center recesses.

To paint the shadow cast from the container and from some lilacs, use Antwerp Blue + Permanent Rose, thin. It may take several layers. Remember that the surface is curving and not flat. Another wash on the upper background was applied to make the lilacs closer in value. Use mixes of Antwerp Blue + Permanent Rose. Wet the paper from the top into the lilacs before applying color.

Tulips and Raspberry Tea

The container is a particular favorite of mine because of the divisions in the shape. These tulips were sent to me as a gift and it seemed appropriate to include the bow in the still life as well as the tea that I enjoyed as I arranged the flowers.

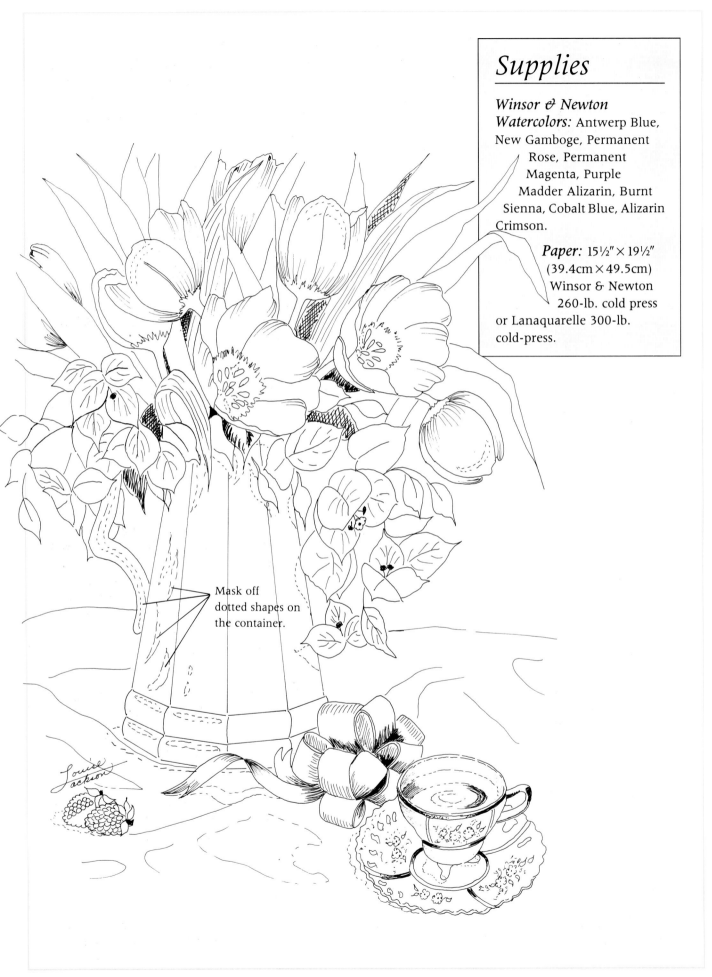

Supplies

*Winsor & Newton
Watercolors:* Antwerp Blue,
New Gamboge, Permanent
Rose, Permanent
Magenta, Purple
Madder Alizarin, Burnt
Sienna, Cobalt Blue, Alizarin
Crimson.

Paper: 15½″ × 19½″
(39.4cm × 49.5cm)
Winsor & Newton
260-lb. cold press
or Lanaquarelle 300-lb.
cold-press.

Mask off
dotted shapes on
the container.

Begin on white paper. When you paint without a wet stage, you may begin with any area you choose. If you are copying a piece of work for a learning experience, it is easiest to apply the first stage to all areas. This will allow drying time without the bother of a hair dryer. This painting is large enough so you will constantly have a place to work while the last area you painted is drying.

TABLECLOTH

Wet the cloth as you would for a wet stage and begin folds by painting in a variation of colors. Use Purple Madder Alizarin thin. Use Cobalt Blue as well as a mix of Antwerp Blue + Permanent Rose to a blue. Add the blue mix as it dries to deepen the folds with Antwerp Blue + Permanent Rose. Control it by using a thirsty brush to keep picking up the color (as it bleeds) to the white high areas of the rolls on the cloth. As this dries and you continue to check the value of your painting against the original, you may continue to deepen the folds with more layers.

OPEN TULIPS

Wet one petal at a time. Leave a white area near the center. Apply a small area of Permanent Rose just near the white. Paint out from that with Permanent Magenta. Add in a little Purple Madder Alizarin for darks. When dry, accent some edges on the sides of the petals with a layer of Alizarin Crimson.

TULIP STAMENS

Paint each shape with New Gamboge. Paint Burnt Sienna down the left side. Cast shadows are purple made with Antwerp Blue + Permanent Rose. Leave the area around the white paper.

The three tulips closest to the open ones are painted again one petal at a time. The light value is Permanent Magenta and the dark is Purple Madder Alizarin. Leave a little white at the base of the flowers. Let this appear to have a jagged edge by applying the paint in a zigzag manner next to the white. The tulips that are left are again painted wet. This time use only a Purple Madder Alizarin to keep them very dull.

STEMS

Base with thin New Gamboge, and shade left side with a green mix of Antwerp Blue + Burnt Sienna.

SMALL FLOWERS

These are bougainvillea. The ones on the right side are lighter, brighter and have more contrast and detail. Paint the lightest petals with a wash of Permanent Rose. When dry, shade the vein area with Permanent Magenta. The stronger red petals were painted thinly with a wash of Alizarin Crimson. When dry, shade with a mix of Alizarin Crimson + Purple Madder Alizarin.

RIBBON

Keep the white areas by painting around them or masking the strong whites. Do what is easiest for you.

On each loop you have a light area. Outside that on both sides of the light is a medium value. Apply the medium value all the way into the dark area. Allow this to dry, then apply the darks and blend to remove the transition lines. Use two different colors for the medium value. Use Permanent Rose on some and Permanent Magenta on others. This gives you variety as well as temperature change. For the darks use Purple Madder Alizarin, and on some use Purple Madder Alizarin + Alizarin Crimson.

SHADOWS

Make the shadows transparent. Use Antwerp Blue + Permanent Rose, or Antwerp Blue + Permanent Rose + New Gamboge. This is a little duller. You may lean some mixes to the warm and some to the cool to create variety. Soften the edges of the shadows slightly with a damp brush. The shadows lean to the color of the object they fall on in this piece. The shadows on the right side of the white vase are warm, reflecting the color of the flowers casting them.

FINISHING DETAIL ON THE TEACUP

Paint a wash of Permanent Magenta on the right side of the tea. This will give it a raspberry cast. Paint tiny flower shapes on the cup of Permanent Rose + a little Permanent Magenta. Add thin dabs of green mix of Antwerp Blue + Burnt Sienna for foliage. Add in a few darks. Paint on dark brown to finish the gold look on the handle and edge of saucer on the right side. Mix brown with New Gamboge + Permanent Magenta + Antwerp Blue.

RASPBERRIES

Paint the one in back with a lavender-blue color. Use Antwerp Blue + Permanent Rose. Paint the one on the right with Permanent Magenta, and use the lavender-blue mix at the bottom to create form. Base the tiny leaves with green. I chose to use white for the raspberry detail because it made it easier, and transparency was not of importance in this small area.

Use a small no. 10 chisel blender brush to pick up white on about five hairs on the corner of the damp brush. Touch the brush to a damp paper towel. Begin at the outside of the berry and paint small *c* shapes. Do several rows on one side. Repeat on the other side. Add white highlights to the circles. Side load this white to separate the tiny leaves. Paint a shadow under.

CENTERS OF BOUGAINVILLEA

Create one white center by painting around it. Paint the rest with Alizarine Crimson + Purple Madder Alizarin. On the left side, use the tulip colors to paint them. Keep them a little quieter and duller.

LEAVES

Paint leaf shapes with variations of green mixes. A few have a wash of New Gamboge. Paint on a blue-violet layer creating more leaves by painting the negative space. This will allow many of the leaves to remain blue-violet. Use a mix of Antwerp Blue + Permanent Rose for this. When leaves are dry, paint another veil of color to create texture and veins. Keep those near the open tulips and keep the lightest area of the container the most detailed.

WHITE OCTAGON VASE

Mask off the small shapes on your drawing. Paint a layer of a gray made with a mix of Antwerp Blue +

Permanent Rose + New Gamboge to the right panel. Leave the second panel white except for the bottom rolled areas. Base these with the gray mix + water.

The far left panel is the darkest, so use a gray mix + less water. Paint the one next to it slightly lighter. Allow each panel to dry before painting next to it. Paint the handle the darkest gray. When dry, remove the masking and apply a thin veil of color overall on the two left panels and handle. When this is dry, soften the edges.

TEACUP

Mask off the tiny white shapes on the saucer. Paint a wash of New Gamboge on the tea. Paint some yellow to the right, sunny side of the saucer. Shade the teacup with a layer to the left side with gray. Paint all of the gold trim with New Gamboge. Shade the teacup with the gray mix. Use Antwerp Blue + Permanent Rose + New Gamboge. Refer to drawing for shading. Paint a gray wash over the left panel and left side of the circle the cup sits on. Make a brown-gold mix of Antwerp Blue + Permanent Rose + New Gamboge. Paint this in the darkest area on the gold trim, and pull the edge out to fade it. Use this mix to shade dark areas of the tea.

FINAL STEP ON CONTAINER

Remove all masking fluid and soften the edges. Paint a thin wash of Cobalt Blue over all white on the two left panels. Add a few strong dark areas to the tulip area. You could add leaves, tulip shapes and/or negative shapes.

1 Wet the paper from the table line down. Apply color to the deepest area of the cloth folds. Soften edges and direct the color with a damp, thirsty brush.

2 Begin painting the tulips by wetting each petal, applying the color and directing it with a thirsty brush. Reserve the white area inside the flower by keeping out the color.

3 Paint on a few leaves. The long ones are simply a long brushstroke of color. The small ones are more controlled. Apply color to one side of the leaf. Blend it and allow it to dry. Complete the other side.

4 Paint washes of color on the container. Because each section has a rather defined edge, it is an easy container to paint.

5 The Bougainvillaea is a wonderful vining type of flower with nice, strong color and well-defined shapes. It has a shape similar to the Japanese Lantern flower, so the petals overlap. Simply change the values of the front and back petals as you see them in the painting.

6 Add some New Gamboge to a few leaves as a base coat and in the center stamen area.

7 Define more leaves, allowing some yellow to show through the green.

8 Add yellow washes to the trim of the cup and saucer. Begin to paint the ribbon.

9 Paint a yellow wash as the first layer on the tea.

10 Paint a wash on the upper background. Paint positive leaves in a variety of values.

11 Continue painting the elements and enjoy the process of being able to move to a new area when you are so inclined. Paint in the duller shadow tulip when the leaves are complete.

12 Deepen some folds on the table, continue painting the ribbon and deepen the color of the tea. Paint the form and shadows on the cup and saucer.

13 Paint a reddish wash on the tea to give it a raspberry tint. Paint the flower and leaf design on the cup and saucer. Add a raspberry or two.

14 Complete ribbon and add shadows.

15 Add shadows from the container. Then add a wash over the strong reflections on the side.

Assortment With Roses

Supplies

Winsor & Newton Watercolors: Naples Yellow, New Gamboge, Permanent Rose, Permanent Magenta, Purple Madder Alizarin, Cobalt Blue, Antwerp Blue, Winsor Violet, Burnt Sienna, Indigo.

Paper: 11" × 22" (27.9cm × 55.9cm) Lanaquarelle 300-lb. cold-press.

This painting is meant to have the look of an assortment of garden flowers. The use of tiny flower shapes peeking out behind others adds to that illusion.

This technique is a combination of painting the first and second values on the flowers in one wet step. The final dark is layered on some objects while others remain less detailed and complete after the first stage. It may require a little practice, especially the roses. You may choose to follow the drawing of all the rose petals, or trace only the outer lines and develop your own rose.

The overall design is called a *cruciform*, which means that it forms a cross. The small darks that help create that shape are important to paint in.

1 Wet the paper all except for the two large roses. Mix Antwerp Blue + Permanent Rose to a blue-violet. Paint this from the outside edges inward. Allow it to bleed into the flowers but don't attempt to cover them all. The idea here is to paint some background that you can still paint over. The background color will be there, and you won't have to paint around all of the tiny filler flowers. Dry this stage.

2 Wet the large rose. This will be white, so paint in just a few strokes of color. Paint in Naples Yellow to the center. Then mix Naples Yellow + tiny amount of Purple Madder Alizarin to get a peachy-pink. Paint triangles and a few *c* strokes.

3 To paint the peach roses, wet your no. 8 round with wet Naples Yellow, and on the very tip of the brush pick up a tiny bit of Permanent Rose. Wipe the excess paint off the tip on the edge of your palette. Use the belly of the brush on the petal, with the Permanent Rose aimed to the outside edge. Continue around the outside, then place a few strokes in the same fashion inside. The pink color will suggest the outside of some petals. Do not be distressed if it doesn't look much like a rose at this point.

Base the wild rose under the white rose with Permanent Magenta, then charge in or stroke on some Purple Madder Alizarin as the dark value. The one to the left of the white rose is a little different. First paint Perma-

nent Rose on the outside edge, then paint on the large mid-value of Permanent Magenta. Then stroke on thicker Purple Madder Alizarin for the dark.

The petal that rolls back under the white rose has a little Permanent Rose along the top edge. Fill the rest with Permanent Magenta, and use Purple Madder Alizarin to the area near the stem and near the rose. I intentionally did not complete them at this point so you could see each petal better.

For leaf colors use Cobalt Blue + Naples Yellow for light leaves and Antwerp Blue + Burnt Sienna for dark leaves. Paint the top ones light and charge in some dark. Paint the one to the right of the rose Naples Yellow with a very dark base. Paint a dark one near the bottom of the rose.

For the zinnia, paint the stroke shapes with Permanent Magenta. Paint four or five strokes, then paint in the dark with Purple Madder Alizarin. While the petals are still wet, paint in Naples Yellow to the center. Let it run.

4 Start the filler flower. Begin at the outer tip of the cluster. Use the tip of the no. 8 round to paint on small oval strokes to be suggestions of leaves with a mix of Cobalt Blue + Naples Yellow. As you move down the stem, paint on several dabs of water. Quickly paint on thin Purple Madder Alizarin as pink blossoms, the same shape as the leaves. Charge in some darker strokes of the same color. Alternate with more leaves, then more flowers down the stem.

Paint in the beard of the iris with New Gamboge and allow to dry. Base one petal with a wash of Permanent Magenta, then streak in the dark value with a mix of Winsor Violet + Indigo. Keep the small petals that come up at the sides light. Paint the stem Naples Yellow at the top and Antwerp Blue + Burnt Sienna.

Paint in the small wild rose at the right with Permanent Magenta, charge in Purple Madder Alizarin for the dark. Paint the center with Naples Yellow.

The tiny flowers above this are based with Permanent Magenta. Use tiny amounts of Permanent Rose to the top of front petals. Add leaves as you go with the two mixes. Notice the dark small leaves above the white roses, and the tiny dark piece of background to the right (this is Indigo + Winsor Violet). These tiny darks will help the white rose appear white.

5 Paint a small flower under the white rose by basing it with thin Permanent Rose, and charge in Purple Madder Alizarin. Use Naples Yellow to the center. Then develop the leaves and stems by layering, drying and painting the negative space. Use the regular green mixes. To shade a couple leaves, use a gray mix of Antwerp Blue + Burnt Sienna + Winsor Violet. Keep it on the light side. Base in the lower right zinnia the same as the other. Paint in several values of long leaves to the right.

6 Paint on the background close to the flowers and leaves. As you come out into the background, blend the edge of color. The reason for this is to cover any very light areas that are left, as well as to paint a layer around the white daisies. Use a mix of Antwerp Blue + Winsor Violet. Continue to fill in more leaves. Add more pink flowers with Permanent Rose and more small blue-violet ones, lighter than before. The iris is a little bluer this time. Use a mix of Antwerp Blue +

Winsor Violet for the base, and use a mix of Antwerp Blue + Winsor Violet and Indigo for the dark value.

Paint in more Purple Madder Alizarin to the small wild roses to strengthen the dark area near the center. Paint a wash of New Gamboge on the center, and add dots of Purple Madder Alizarin and Winsor Violet around the center. The large flower under the white rose has a wash of Permanent Rose painted on the front petal to make it a little brighter.

The rose at the right has the next layer on it, while the one on the left is complete. The next layer is to define some of the rolled petals by painting small shapes under them and in small triangles at the corner under petals. Use a mix of Naples Yellow + Purple Madder Alizarine. Use the same on the white rose but very little and very thin. Also use a mix of Antwerp Blue + Winsor Violet on the right side, mostly of the white one. Paint in New Gamboge to the center, and add some Purple Madder Alizarin for pollen, allowing

it to bleed. Soften the edges, especially on the white rose. I chose to add some leaves falling on the peach rose on the left to tuck it into the bouquet.

I used a round brush with a good point on it to paint in some swooping, loose strokes around the outside of the design. Use a light green mix for this. You may want to practice first. After softening the edges of the daisies, I decided to leave them white with no shading because the white helped balance the rose.

7 Adjust the flowers by painting in stronger darks to the roses. Use Purple Madder Alizarin on the peach-colored roses. Your eye should pull into the white and peach rose. Darken tiny darks around the white rose. Keep the white rose delicate by not adding strong darks in the actual rose.

I chose to roll an edge or two by painting on Antwerp Blue + Winsor Violet on the edge. I wanted to keep some lost edges on the left side of the rose. If any petals need to be lightened, simply lift out the color with a soft brush. If you are using the Lanaquarelle paper, remember that it is so soft that it does not scrub well. It is best to gently loosen the pigment and blot.

These roses have rolling petals. If you show every one they get very busy. I felt the irises paled at this point, so I painted a layer of Winsor Violet over the dark areas of both irises to brighten them up. There is an iris that was added to the extreme left. Don't let it get dark. Paint in a base with thin Antwerp Blue + Winsor Violet. Add in a little dark with a thin Winsor Violet + Indigo. It just suggests the flower with no detail.

I lived with the painting for a day and decided it needed a little more tying together. I added a few more small flowers in the lower left area and two dark burgundy zinnias. For the zinnias, use Purple Madder Alizarin. Lift out some color where the tops of the small petals would start before applying the burgundy.

1 To achieve some light values of color behind all of the small flowers, it is best to paint those first in the wet stage. Wet around the white roses and leave them dry and white. After painting the colors listed for the wet stage, dry the paper. Wet the roses and paint a few strokes of color (see text, page 118). This will provide a starting point for the roses.

2 Painting the flowers with a base of one color and charging in the dark value is easy and effective even over a lightly painted background.

3 Continue to create the small flowers. Paint leaf shapes and flower centers as well. (Directions for these are in Step Three. You may also refer to the flower worksheet.)

4 As the filler flowers reach out toward the edges of the design, they need to be similar in value and temperature to recede. They also need to have less detail on them. Directions for this stage are listed in Step four.

This flower worksheet shows the
first layer of the small flowers.
Allow this to dry as you work on
others. Following the directions,
you will go back to paint the front
side on some and the center
shading.

5 Develop the small pink flower between the roses, then begin to layer the leaves. Use a variety of values. Allow each layer to dry. Position the leaves in a variety of directions. With each layer get a little darker until you have a couple very dark leaves. Paint a few tiny, dark negative shapes. You may need to darken the background as well.

6 Wet the background down as far as the flowers, and deepen the outer edges as well as any areas that remained white from the first wet stage. Continue adding more flowers as directed in Step six. Begin creating the rolled petals on the peach roses with a mix of Naples Yellow + Purple Madder Alizarin. Paint small triangles at the corners under petals. When you blend the transition line, this will separate the petals. To separate the petals on the white flower, use more water in your mixes to keep it light.

7 Continue to fill with leaves and refine the small flowers. Paint as many layers on the roses as it takes to roll the petals. Each of us may use a different amount of water when applying the paint so it will take us a different number of layers to accomplish the same result.

Index

More Great Books for Decorative Painters!

Acrylic Decorative Painting Techniques—Discover stroke-by-stroke instruction that takes you through the basics and beyond! More than 50 fun and easy painting techniques are illustrated in simple demonstrations that offer at least two variations on each method. Plus, a thorough discussion on tools, materials, color, preparation and backgrounds. *#30884/$24.99/128 pages/550 color illus.*

Painting & Decorating Birdhouses—Turn unfinished birdhouses into something special—from a quaint Victorian roost to a Southwest pueblo, from a rustic log cabin to a lighthouse! These colorful and easy decorative painting projects are for the birds with 22 clever projects to create indoor decorative birdhouses, as well as functional ones to grace your garden. *#30882/$23.99/128 pages/194 color illus./paperback*

Decorative Painting Sourcebook—Priscilla Hauser, Phillip Myer and Jackie Shaw lend their expertise to this one-of-a-kind guide straight from the pages of *Decorative Artist's Workbook!* You'll find step-by-step, illustrated instructions on every technique—from basic brushstrokes to faux finishes, painting glassware, wood, clothing and much more! *#30883/$24.99/128 pages/200 color illus./paperback*

The Decorative Stamping Sourcebook—Embellish walls, furniture, fabric and accessories—with stamped designs! You'll find 180 original, traceable motifs in a range of themes and illustrated instructions for making your own stamps to enhance any decorating style. *#30898/$24.99/128 pages/200 color illus.*

Master Strokes—Master the techniques of decorative painting with this comprehensive guide! Learn to use decorative paint finishes on everything from small objects and furniture to walls and floors, including dozens of step-by-step demonstrations and numerous techniques. *#30937/$22.99/160 pages/400 color illus./paperback*

The Best of Silk Painting—Discover inspiration in sophisticated silk with this gallery of free-flowing creativity. Over 100 full-color photos capture the glorious colors, unusual textures and unique designs of 77 talented artists. *#30840/$29.99/128 pages/136 color illus.*

Painting Houses, Cottages and Towns on Rocks—Discover how a dash of paint can turn humble stones into charming cottages, churches, Victorian mansions and more. This hands-on, easy-to-follow book offers a menagerie of fun—and potentially profitable—stone animal projects. Eleven examples, complete with material list, photos of the finished piece and patterns will help you create entire rock villages. *#30823/$21.99/128 pages/398 color illus./paperback*

Decorative Painting With Gretchen Cagle—Discover decorative painting at its finest as you browse through pages of charm-

ing motifs. You'll brighten walls, give life to old furniture, create unique accent pieces and special gifts using step-by-step instructions, traceable drawings, detailed color mixes and more! *#30803/$24.99/144 pages/64 color, 36 b&w illus./paperback*

Creative Paint Finishes for Furniture—Revive your furniture with fresh color and design! Inexpensive, easy and fun painting techniques are at your fingertips, along with step-by-step directions and a photo gallery of imaginative applications for faux finishing, staining, stenciling, mosaic, découpage and many other techniques. *#30748/$27.99/144 pages/236 color, 7 b&w illus.*

Creative Paint Finishes for the Home—A complete, full-color step-by-step guide to decorating floors, walls and furniture—including how to use the tools, master the techniques and develop ideas. *#30426/$27.99/144 pages/212 color illus.*

Master Works: How to Use Paint Finishes to Transform Your Surroundings—Discover how to use creative paint finishes to enhance and excite the "total look" of your home. This step-by-step guide contains dozens of exciting ideas on fresco, marbling, paneling and other simple paint techniques for bringing new life to any space. Plus, you'll also find innovative uses for fabrics, screens and blinds. *#30626/$29.95/176 pages/150 color illus.*

Create Your Own Greeting Cards and Gift Wrap with Priscilla Hauser—You'll see sponge prints, eraser prints, cellophane scrunching, marbleizing, paper making and dozens of other techniques you can use to make unique greetings for all your loved ones. *#30621/$24.99/128 pages/230 color illus.*

Stencil Source Book 2—Add color and excitement to fabrics, furniture, walls and more with over 200 original motifs that can be used again and again! Idea-packed chapters will help you create dramatic color schemes and themes to enhance your home in hundreds of ways. *#30730/$22.99/144 pages/300 illus.*

The Crafts Supply Sourcebook, 4th edition—Turn here to find the materials you need—from specialty tools and the hardest-to-find accessories, to clays, doll parts, patterns, quilting machines and hundreds of other items! Listings organized by area of interest make it quick and easy! *#70344/$18.99/320 pages/paperback*

Paint Craft—Discover great ideas for enhancing your home, wardrobe and personal items. You'll see how to master the basics of mixing and planning colors, how to print with screen and linoleum to create your own stationery, how to enhance old glassware and pottery pieces with unique patterns and motifs and much more! *#30678/$16.95/144 pages/200 color illus./paperback*

Nature Craft—Dozens of step-by-step nature craft projects to create, including dried flower garlands, baskets, corn dollies, potpourri and more. Bring the outdoors inside with these wonderful projects crafted with readily available natural materials. *#30531/$16.99/144 pages/200 color illus./paperback*

Paper Craft—Dozens of step-by-step paper craft projects to make, including greeting cards, boxes and desk sets, jewelry and pleated paper blinds. If you have ever worked with or wanted to work with paper you'll enjoy these attractive, fun-to-make projects. *#30530/$16.95/144 pages/200 color illus./paperback*

Everything You Ever Wanted to Know About Fabric Painting—Discover how to create beautiful fabrics! You'll learn how to set up work space, choose materials, plus the ins and outs of tie-dye, screen printing, woodgraining, marbling, cyanotype and more! *#30625/$21.99/128 pages/4-color throughout/paperback*

Painting Murals—Learn through eight step-by-step projects how to choose a subject for a mural, select colors that will create the desired effects and transfer the design to the final surface. *#30081/$29.99/168 pages/125 color illus.*

Other fine North Light Books are available from your local bookstore, art supply store, or direct from the publisher. Write to the address below for a FREE catalog of all North Light Books. To order books directly from the publisher, include $3.50 postage and handling for one book, $1.00 for each additional book. Ohio residents add 6% sales tax. Allow 30 days for delivery.

North Light Books
1507 Dana Avenue
Cincinnati, Ohio 45207
VISA/MasterCard orders call TOLL-FREE
1-800-289-0963

Prices subject to change without notice.   Stock may be limited on some books.

Write to this address for information on *The Artist's Magazine*, North Light Books, North Light Book Club, Graphic Design Book Club, North Light Art School, and Betterway Books. To receive information on art or design competitions, send a SASE to Dept. BOI, Attn: Competition Coordinator, at the above address.

8548